Reimagining Worship

Reimagining Worship

Renewing Worship in a Changing Church

Edited by

Anna de Lange
Trevor Lloyd
Tim Stratford
Ian Tarrant

CANTERBURY
PRESS
Norwich

© The Editors and Contributors 2017

First published in 2017 by Canterbury Press

Editorial office
3rd Floor, Invicta House,
108–114 Golden Lane,
London EC1Y OTG.

Canterbury Press is an imprint of Hymns Ancient & Modern Ltd
(a registered charity)
13A Hellesdon Park Road, Norwich,
Norfolk, NR6 5DR.

www.canterburypress.co.uk

British Library Cataloguing in Publication data

A catalogue record for this book is available
from the British Library.

978 1 84825 913 3

Typeset by Regent Typesetting
Printed and bound in Great Britain by
CPI Group (UK) Ltd

CONTENTS

C RESPONDING

D SENDING

CONTRIBUTORS

The contributors are all members of the Group for the Renewal of Worship (GROW), a broadly evangelical bunch of people who for over 45 years have produced a stream of practical and provocative booklets and larger works on worship. Those marked * are members or former members of the Church of England Liturgical Commission.

Revd Patrick Angier, Vicar, St Peter's, Prestbury, Cheshire.

Revd Helen Bent, Praxis and RSCM Head of Ministerial Training. *

Rt Revd Dr Colin Buchanan, retired Bishop. *

Mrs Anna de Lange, Reader, Christ Church, Dore, Sheffield. *

Revd Nick Drake, Theology and Formation Pastor, St Luke's, Gas Street, Birmingham.

Revd Mark Earey, Director of Anglican Formation and Tutor in Liturgy at The Queen's Foundation for Ecumenical Theological Education, Birmingham. *

Mrs Anne Harrison, freelance church musician and editor.

Revd John Leach, Developing Discipleship Adviser and Trainer, Diocese of Lincoln.

The Venerable Trevor Lloyd, retired Archdeacon. *

Revd Dr Daniel Newman, Assistant Curate, parish of Radipole and Melcombe Regis, Weymouth.

Revd Colin Randall, Priest in Charge, Coln River Group, Gloucester.

Revd Charles Read, Director of Liturgy and Worship, Eastern Region Ministry Course; Director of Reader Training and Deputy Warden of Readers, Diocese of Norwich.

Revd Joanna Seabourne, Priest in Charge, St Augustine's, Wrangthorne; Associate Rector, St George's, Leeds.

Revd Liz Simpson, Rector, West Buckingham Benefice, Diocese of Oxford.

Revd Dr James Steven, Academic Dean and Programme Leader for Christian Liturgy, Sarum College.

The Venerable Dr Tim Stratford, Archdeacon of Leicester.*

Revd Matthew Swires-Hennessy, Associate Minister, St Peter's Church, Farnborough.

Canon Ian Tarrant, Rector, St Mary's, Woodford.

Revd Dr Phillip Tovey, Deputy Warden LLM (Licensed Lay Ministry), Diocese of Oxford; Liturgy Tutor, Ripon College, Cuddesdon; Course Leader for the MA in Ministry, Diocese of Oxford – Oxford Brookes University.

Revd John Waller, Rector, Benefice of The Brickhills and Stoke Hammond, Diocese of Oxford.

INTRODUCTION

Reimagining and reshaping:
a prospectus for worship?

What is our worship in the future going to be like? What principles should govern and inspire out worship? Or should it just happen? Or is there no need to think about principles because we have a full text to follow for every season and occasion, provided for the Church of England by *Common Worship*?

We believe the Church should continually be in the business of reformation – re-forming, reshaping, re-visioning not only our worship but the being of the Church itself. Both the Church and our worship should be dynamic, on the move, going somewhere, not static, fossilised, bound by law to the styles of the past. So we have been discussing a range of principles that may determine the character and quality, as well as the content, of our worship in the future.

In almost every human encounter four things happen – two or more people meet, they exchange words (or blows or some other actions as well), they respond to that exchange and they part, go away, depart. Look at what happens in the Gospel encounters Jesus has with people, for instance. It is no coincidence that that is also the structure of the Church's liturgy. We gather, we speak and hear the word, we respond in creed, prayers, sacraments, and we are sent out, dismissed on a mission to the world. So this is the structure of our book, something timeless and enduring, and at the same time both biblical and intensely human.

We begin by looking at the gathering of God's people. Who are they, this kaleidoscopic group of people, with many different routes into their relationship with Jesus Christ, different cultures, ages and backgrounds, different sexual orientation as well as much else? And what does it look like when they meet, in terms of leadership and gifts, numbers and spaces for gathering? As we look to the future, how much of this is going to change? Will the Church change her worship in order to accommodate the changes, or will the worship of the Church, in a spirit-filled encounter with the living God, be what changes the Church?

Then we move from the who to the word, to the content and parameters of that exchange. This, rightly, is the theological bit as we ask what it is for worship, now and in the future, to be biblical, charismatic, trinitarian, christocentric. And how do we enter into this worship? What is the content of the gospel, and how do we hear it and believe, express our faith and doubt? How is all this conveyed, presented, passed on in the tradition, teaching, edifying, building up, growing of the people of God? And what is the end result? Looking at the final judgement or the heavenly banquet brings into the present our sharing in God's view of things, both in rejoicing and in righteousness.

The third section is all about our response, as we look at the relationship between the internal and the external, between the sense of awe, overwhelmed by God's transcendence, and the practical outworking of our response in terms of sacraments, belief and commitment, and the experience – and ministry – of forgiveness and healing. And through it all, often in a non-cerebral way, giving it expression and helping us keep in tune with God, floats music and the sound of silence.

And so we go out, carrying with us the presence of Christ in our behaviour, the way we express our belief and commit ourselves both as individuals and corporately as a Church to God's mission in his world – inspired, dedicated and obedient to his calling to transform that world as we find ourselves being transformed by being in the presence of God both in the Church and in the world.

The list of principles emerging from our discussions is not exhaustive: we have found that listing some of them resulted in us thinking of others, and you will probably want to add more. We offer the principles, patterns and hopes for the future of our worship, not in any prescriptive or definitive way, but to stimulate and provoke church members and leaders to grapple with the principles these issues raise for our worship.

And if the list on the Contents page looks a bit static, too feet-on-the-ground, try tearing it out and turning it sideways, reading it Chinese-style. Make a grid with this list along the top as well as down the side and explore the effect each aspect of worship has on the others – it will give you an agenda for weeks of discussion and it might just blow your mind. Take 'Relational' for instance. What effect does our relationship have on our caring, on our encouraging each other to be creative, on the way we shape our space for worship, the way we teach and learn, the way we encounter God or on our sacramental experience or on our encouraging each other in Christlikeness and in mission? Try this process with the rest. Use it as a tool to analyse and evaluate what is going on in the Church's worship, life and mission, and to set agendas for the future. In this kaleidoscopic, non-linear exploration we will discover that neither *Common Worship* nor any successor is the last word. But we will find threads running through our worship. Everything is connected to everything else. Explore the connections that result in growth, as Paul does with the body in Ephesians 4. Worship is not about taking apart and analysing the dry historical bones of the liturgy but about enabling connections and growth, and watching in awe and wonder, like Ezekiel, as the bones rattle together and come alive, filled with the Spirit. These principles and threads running through our worship are used by the Spirit to give vision and direction to our worship, holding it together, integrating our belief, our humanity, our history and our destiny as those who will gather for worship, overwhelmed by God's presence around a throne in heaven.

Using this book

You can read it in the order in which it is set out, the familiar pattern of the Holy Communion service – Gathering, Word, Sacrament and Going out. You can dip into it anywhere, looking for subjects that interest you or things your church or group is focusing on. As you read, you may like to make a note of things that strike you, that you want to talk to someone about. You will find two things to help this process – questions and links.

Questions

You will find questions scattered throughout the book, to help you think through things or for discussion with others. There are three sorts of questions:

- **To think about** – questions for individual reflection when reading.
- **To discuss** – questions for a home group, leadership group or church council.
- **For the wider Church** – issues of policy and national discussion.

Links

You will also find four icons in the margins, linking together various places in the book where similar themes occur. These are:

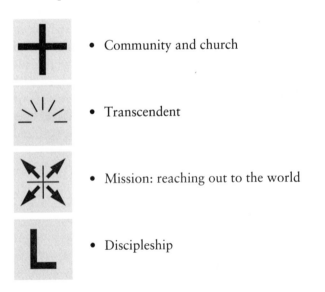

- Community and church

- Transcendent

- Mission: reaching out to the world

- Discipleship

REFERENCES AND ABBREVIATIONS

For ease of reference, throughout the book you will find reference to the following, without the full details which you have here:

ASB   The Alternative Service Book 1980, Oxford University Press, 1980

BCP   The Book of Common Prayer 1662

CHP   Church House Publishing, London (www.chpublishing.co.uk)

CW   *Common Worship: Services and Prayers for the Church of England*, Church House Publishing, 2000

CWCI   *Common Worship: Christian Initiation*, Church House Publishing, 2006

CWPS   *Common Worship: Pastoral Services*, Church House Publishing, 2000

CWDP   *Common Worship: Daily Prayer*, Church House Publishing, 2000

CWTS   *Common Worship: Times and Seasons*, Church House Publishing, 2006

GB   Grove Books Limited, Nottingham and Cambridge (https://grovebooks.co.uk)

GBW   Grove Books Worship Series

GBEv   Grove Books Evangelism Series

JLS   Joint Liturgical Studies, published by Hymns A & M in partnership with the Alcuin Club and the Group for the Renewal of Worship

NPW   *New Patterns for Worship*, Church House Publishing, 2002

RSCM   Royal School of Church Music

'Worship should be ...
or should involve ...'

A:
GATHERING

A1

RELATIONAL

To belong is a powerful and transformative experience; whether it is joining in with the singing of the national anthem at a rugby match, singing along with a live band and thousands of others at a stadium gig, or understanding the culture of your place of work. On a superficial level we show our belonging by carrying membership or loyalty cards, or wearing a particular style of clothing. But relating as part of the Church calls us to deeper engagement and calls us to reject both individualism and tribalism.

> 'The gift of belonging is already ours.'[1]

One of the striking images of the Church found in the New Testament is that of 'the body'. The unity of the body of the Church is found in Christ – one Lord, one faith, one baptism (Eph. 4.5) – but how does, or how can, corporate worship encourage that sense of relating to God and to one another?

TO THINK ABOUT

- Should worship be more than 'me and Jesus'?
- To what extent is your church community made up of 'people like you'?
- How much does our experience of worshipping together look past the divisions of denomination and style and to the unity of the new creation?

---

1 E. Lane, *Lessons in Belonging*, InterVarsity Press, 2015, p. 86.

Biblical authority

The theme of belonging may not be an obvious concept to draw out of the biblical narrative, yet through both Old and New Testaments we observe the strength of people's identity as they discover their belonging, their relationship with God and with one another. Belonging is seen throughout, from the relationship described in the garden of Genesis to the glorious vision of John in Revelation.

Old Testament

The Lord speaks in Ezekiel 37 of raising up a people who will be brought together and cleansed. Key to their identity is their belonging to God: 'they shall be my people, and I will be their God' (Ezek. 37.23).

The people of Israel know what it is to come together for worship, for recommitment and for formation. We hear the joy of the Psalmist's cry, 'I was glad when they said to me, "Let us go to the house of the Lord"' (Ps. 122.1). Not a singular expression of worship and devotion, although they are present, but a joy at joining in with others in the worship of God. This community is formed around the word of God, as we read in Nehemiah, 'all the people gathered together' to hear the words of the Book (Neh. 8.1).

'Israel was a nation constantly being summoned to assemble before the Lord and/or his representatives in times of covenant renewal and national crisis.'[2]

Worship, and spiritual renewal and challenge, is sometimes an individual experience (such as Jacob's Ladder in Genesis 28) but often communal, as the people gather as one and are formed into the people of God (look at Joshua's challenge 'choose this day ...' in Joshua 24.15).

2 R. Reymond, *A New Systematic Theology of the Christian Faith*, Thomas Nelson, 1998, p. 809.

Several psalms act to call people to worship together, encouraging the community to rejoice together in what God has done in them and for them:

O magnify the Lord with me, and let us exalt his name together. (Ps. 34.3)

O come, let us worship and bow down, let us kneel before the Lord our Maker!
For he is our God, and we are the people of his pasture, and the sheep of his hand. (Ps. 95.6–7)

We give thanks to you, O God; we give thanks; your name is near.
People tell of your wondrous deeds. (Ps. 75.1)

There are expressions of how God has come to the rescue of individuals, but there is a clear stream of praise which corporately exhorts the people of God to live in the light of their common faith and identity.

New Testament

The New Testament speaks of a unity which 'knows no geographic, administrative or cultural limits. It is based in Jesus. By his death and resurrection, Jesus opened the way to new alliances for all peoples, who had formerly been without grace and were enemies of God. Through faith in Jesus, the believer is part of a new nation, reconciled to God'.[3]

The Apostle Paul encourages the church in Ephesus to strive to keep that unity found in their common faith, 'making every effort to maintain the unity of the Spirit in the bond of peace. There is one body and one Spirit, just as you were called to the one hope of your calling, one Lord, one faith, one baptism, one God and Father of all, who is above all and through all and in all' (Eph. 4.3–6).

3 K. Kosse, 'Unity of Believers', in T. Adeyemo (ed.), *Africa Bible Commentary*, Zondervan, 2006, p. 1288.

Jesus prays in John 17 for the unity of those who would later believe: 'I ask not only on behalf of these, but also on behalf of those who will believe in me through their word, that they may all be one. As you, Father, are in me and I am in you' (John 17.20–21). Again, there is an expectation that the community of faith is rooted in belief in Jesus and there is desire that the relationships within that community of shared faith would be unified as Father and Son are known in unity. This, therefore, is not a call to identikit Christians, but to a community with love for one another, and a unity of purpose.

Meeting together

The church is to be a fellowship of worshippers. The early chapters of Acts speak of teaching, prayers, breaking bread, and practical action. The Corinthian church needed to be reminded that members should not be selfish when meeting together to celebrate the Lord's Supper (1 Cor. 11), and Hebrews 10.25 is a call to meet together, not to focus exclusively on individual discipleship, 'not neglecting to meet together, as is the habit of some, but encouraging one another, and all the more as you see the Day approaching'.

We belong to God

As we meet together, we share a common confession: Jesus is Lord. That shared faith needs to be restated, so that our meeting together encourages each believer in their faith.

It is important that there is individual faith, but perhaps it is more important when meeting together that our corporate identity is as those who belong to the Lord. We need to rejoice in our identity as God's people as we come together in worship and as we recognize our fellowship together. In other words, we need to hold to both the significance of *ecclesia*, that is of assembly, and of *kyriakos*, those who belong to the Lord. It has reportedly been said that without faith the Church is like Rotary with a spire. The difference in quality of having a common faith in Christ should bring about a greater sense of belonging.

We belong to one another – local, national and international

The *local* church is a sign of community in a world that longs for connection, belonging, authenticity and interaction. We are called to relate to one another as sisters and brothers in Christ. This sign, as long as it is coupled with a firm understanding of our common belonging to God, should be a powerful witness in the world.

> '... the overwhelming majority of references to the church [in the New Testament] are to a local, living and loving collection of people who are committed to Christ and committed to one another.'[4]

Most churches still retain a very local nature, and this can be particularly true of churches in more rural areas. They aim to reflect their local area in terms of variation of age and demographics and see this as a strength for mission rather than trying to be a homogeneous unit.[5]

Other churches gather their congregations from a wide geographical area, and yet others meet at weekends on deserted industrial estates. Worshippers are not just bound together by geography, but they are a visible sign of the presence of God within a particular community.

TO THINK ABOUT

- Does the congregation you attend try to reflect its locality? How can you know if it has succeeded?
- Do you feel you have to conform to a certain standard of living or education to be welcomed?

The *national* Church is a reminder of wider fellowship, and ideally should engender mutual support and encouragement. The

---

4 M. Denver, *Nine Marks of a Healthy Church*, Crossway, 2004, p. 149.
5 For more on this, see A2 Caring and Inclusive.

New Testament tells of the concern of those Christians living far away from Jerusalem for the church there, for its wellbeing. We also see letters addressed to churches in a particular region rather than just to one specific congregation. Belonging to a denomination or network is a reminder to a local church that they are part of something bigger than themselves. This can be helpful in inspiring smaller congregations who may feel isolated, and helpful for larger congregations who think they are the only ones doing kingdom work!

TO THINK ABOUT

- What would it look like if your congregation linked to another in a different situation, maybe in terms of rural vs urban, or suburban vs council estate?
- Would this encourage a greater sense of belonging to the body of Christ?

Relating to others on a national scale, perhaps to a denomination, could be something that becomes less important in coming years, although there is a value to connecting with others even though they are different in many ways. On the other hand, churches might connect more through alternative networks and oversight, which give the opportunity for non-local support without the same level of permanence and structure.

We are inspired to remember the *international* dimension of the Church by the vision of worship in Revelation 7. It includes those of every tribe and tongue and nation. While some churches are easily reminded of this by the presence of diverse cultural groups within congregations, others can struggle to see beyond their own experience. Support of mission organizations and links to other dioceses within the Anglican Communion can help this sense of belonging, but often these things do not make a meaningful difference to the worshipping life of a congregation. On the other hand it is entirely possible to use liturgical resources and music from other nations and Anglican Provinces.

New ways of belonging

The Church Army Research Unit has devised a series of questions in order to help them identify Fresh Expressions of Church. The very first question speaks of the group being 'Christian and communal'.[6]

'The Way' in Carlisle is a group of young adults that has grown out of a student dinners initiative, as Matthew Firth, the minister, explains:

> The Way on Wednesday follows on from student dinners and it's a key point of gathering for our community during the week. It's a mixed group of Christians and non-Christians and it's a gathering where people can start to explore the Christian faith, perhaps for the first time. We use all sorts of methods, we use bits of student Alpha, we use creative arts, we explore spirituality and prayer in different ways and it's been really great to have Johnny [a non-Christian student] helping out with leading some of the sessions and bringing a really fresh approach to things. But, as well as that, we've found it's been really important for the Christian members of The Way to gather together on a Sunday evening for worship and prayer and teaching. And we also gather around a Communion meal and we found that this gathering has really become the fuel for the whole spiritual life of the community.

This staged approach places relationships at the beginning and at the heart of worship. The strength of The Way seems to be creating spaces and experiences flowing from relationships rather than trying to connect people once they have arrived at, say, a church service.[7]

---

6 Church Army Research Unit report on Guildford Diocese: www.cofeguildford.org.uk/about/pde/church-health-growth/fresh-expressions (accessed 25 June 2015).

7 Fresh Expressions Stories: www.freshexpressions.org.uk/stories/theway/jan15 (accessed 25 June 2015).

Making connections online through social media and other interactive platforms is, for many, a part of everyday life. *i-church* describes itself as an 'online Christian community based on Benedictine principles' and was founded by the Anglican Diocese of Oxford.[8] The 'chatroom-Chapel' hosts services and there are online resources to aid individual devotion. This, of course, raises questions about the nature of online versus offline relationships and whether a wholly-online Christian experience offers a healthy discipleship. Perhaps online communities are not to replace existing forms of church, but to complement or perhaps provide an accessible expression of Christianity to the spiritual seeker. Nicola David, who runs *Church on the Net*, sees it as 'a stepping stone to real life church'.[9]

TO THINK ABOUT

- Even if the church you go to does currently have a fresh expression, how could the model of communal sharing positively impact the life of the congregation you attend?
- In inherited models of church are we asking too much of 'Sunday' corporate worship? Should more emphasis be placed on relationships being developed and strengthened by small groups, courses, social events and mentoring?
- In a world that longs for authentic relationships, should churches invest in online communities?

For more on Fresh Expressions, see Matt Stone, *Fresh Expressions of Church*, GBEv 92, 2010; Tim Sumpter, *Freshly Expressed Church*, GBEv 109, 2015.

---

8 www.i-church.org/gatehouse/.

9 M. Casserly, *What happened to online churches?*, www.christiantoday.com/article/what.happened.to.online.churches/54701.htm (accessed 25 June 2015).

How does this work out in practice?

There are several things that can help or hinder this sense of relating to God together, and relating to the Church (local, national, and global). As Parker Palmer puts it: 'Belonging is not a set of feelings we depend on but a set of practices we enact'.[10]

TO DISCUSS

• Could you work through the points that follow with those who lead corporate worship in the congregation you attend, or with the wider church leadership?

I vs We

The language that is used in our prayers, songs and hymns speaks strongly of our identity as a congregation. One good thing about *Common Worship* is that it makes corporate the regular language of the spoken liturgy. Saying 'I believe' is helpful in challenging our individual discipleship but 'We believe' speaks more clearly of our joint journey of discipleship. Many contemporary songs seem to be written as personal expressions of praise and worship, or for an album, and then find their way into use in the church, which means they often employ 'I' rather than 'We'. This is not only a recent issue: just consider 'When I survey'!

TO THINK ABOUT

• When we are praying together or affirming our faith, are we using appropriate language?
• Does the language used help to form our identity as the body of Christ – 'though we are many, we are one body'?
• Do our songs encourage individualism or seek to help the congregation speak to one another in 'psalm, hymns and spiritual songs'?

10 P. Palmer, 'Foreword', in E. Lane, *Lessons in Belonging*, Inter-Varsity Press, 2015, p. 10.

'Making my communion' vs Together worshipping God

It is not just the language of corporate worship that can help and hinder our sense of belonging. There is a problem if the music is so loud it does not need my voice and the lights are so low I cannot see my fellow believers, for then how do I feel as if I belong in anything more than a superficial sense (like singing along with a band at a gig)? The design of our worship spaces often leads to an 'us and them' separation, whether it is by raised staging, a mass of microphone stands, chancel steps or rood screens. These barriers do little to encourage a sense of belonging together. In a similar way a more traditional, perhaps eight o'clock BCP service, mentality of 'making my communion' and not making eye contact with anyone else can also make it difficult to 'belong'. (For more on the effect of church buildings, see A4 Located.)

This non-verbal side of worship might cause us to think critically about services with prayer stations or different responses during sung worship. As Lily Lewin writes: 'That's why I love experiential worship and believe it makes sense. Everyone gets to engage in worshipping God on their own time and in their own way'.[11]

TO THINK ABOUT

• Does our corporate worship require participation?
• How important is fellowship as part of worship?
• How can we balance giving space for individual response with creating community?

Establishing intent vs confused purpose

The opening of an act of worship should signal its intended direction, in terms of relationship to both God and one another. *Common Worship*'s Service of the Word and Morning Prayer begin with Preparation, and Holy Communion with The

11 L. Lewin, 'Atmosphere, Architecture and Participation', in J. Baker (ed.), *Curating Worship*, SPCK, 2010, p. 159.

Gathering. They speak from the start of the church community gathering for a particular purpose and rooted in common faith.

Look at a few recent reports on the Mystery Worshipper part of the Ship of Fools website. Focus on the comments about the welcome (before, during and after the service). What strikes you about the variety of responses? Then imagine visiting the church you go to, and answering some of the questions posed by the reports. If you are brave enough, ask someone to come to your church as a mystery worshipper, and test out if you have been right in your assessment.

TO THINK ABOUT

- What were the exact opening words of last Sunday's service?
- How well does the opening of worship focus on the intent, and speak of worship as a corporate activity?
- Are there advantages in opening with words of scripture?
- Should corporate worship of the body of Christ begin with the words 'Good Morning' / 'Good Evening'?

Praying for other congregations vs Praying for our own congregation

One pastor writes:

'Every Sunday morning, I lead the congregation of Third Avenue Baptist Church in a 'pastoral prayer'. I pray for many things during that time – congregational events, members who are suffering, evangelistic opportunities, various officials in government, missions opportunities, even events in the nation's headlines. The part of the prayer that elicits the most comment, however – both positive and out of sheer confusion – is when I pray for another evangelical church or two meeting in the city of Louisville.'[12]

---

12 Greg Gilbert, *Why I pray publicly for other churches*, http://thegospelcoalition.org/blogs/tgc/2013/06/26/why-i-pray-publicly-for-other-churches/ (accessed 25 June 2015).

Including other churches as well as the more general world in our prayers reminds us of the mission that we share with them.[13]

TO THINK ABOUT

- How far do our prayers reach?
- Are people invited to contribute things for prayer during the service?
- Do our prayers model our belonging to the wider Church?

Singing songs from various sources vs One hymn book or all home-grown songs

If all of our songs are from one particular stable then it is unlikely we will experience the richness of the diversity of the kingdom of God within our sung worship. As we belong to a better connected Church, as a result of technology, it is easier to access musical resources from the global Church. Placing on our lips words and melodies written by Christians who are persecuted or who live in war-torn troubled countries encourages a greater sense of belonging to the world-wide Church. (For more on this see C8 Musical.)

TO THINK ABOUT

- How often do we sing something that is written outside a white-Western context?
- What are the themes that are missing from our songs and hymns?
- Is our worship shaped by the priorities of our community, or by the latest worship album, or by what the cathedral is singing?

---

13 For more on prayer and intercessions, see C5 Intercessory, and Anna de Lange and Liz Simpson, *How to Lead the Prayers*, GBW 169, 2002.

Established liturgy vs Constant invention

The familiar refrains of opening responses or prayers of thanksgiving can help establish a group together. If a traditional prayer is used, even the Lord's Prayer, there is a sense of remembering what has gone before, and of a shared history. This shared history does not necessarily need traditional language, but a sense of the rhythm of what has been prayed by congregations in the past. The constant introduction of new texts can hinder a congregation carrying some of the phrases of corporate prayer into their private devotions, although some new texts help to challenge and enliven faith.

TO THINK ABOUT

In the church you go to:

• Do the texts of the liturgy change so often that people find it hard to join in?
• If texts are projected, have people enough time to think before they have to speak?
• Does the pattern of the worship help to encourage belonging?
• Who is looking out for good new texts?

Regular sharing/testimony vs Only pre-scripted text and sermons

As part of sharing together in worship it is good to hear what God is doing in the lives of individuals and the life of the church. Stories of what God is doing now highlight the fact that we belong to a living body, not a historical society. Giving opportunity for people to praise God and give thanks for those who journey with them encourages the congregation as a whole to see their role as not simply a passive one. Even the time of giving the notices can speak of the life that we experience as God's children together, rather than simply announcing what events are coming up on the church calendar. Why not take the opportunity to report back to adults about children's activities, to children about what the adults have been doing, from evangelistic courses and from significant events in the church's life? Doing this as part of corporate worship helps to encourage a sense of belonging and participation. (For more on sermons and handling the word of God see chapters in Section B.)

TO THINK ABOUT

- How do we provide opportunities for congregations to share life in the context of worship?
- Can we tell the stories that speak of belonging and community in worship and more widely?
- Is there opportunity to hear the stories and voices of believers from different contexts and countries as part of our worship?

Why it matters

'Yet, the battle for the Church would be won or lost not in monastic communities, but out in the secular world: the parishes of the two provinces.'[14]

This comment about sixteenth-century England is still true in contemporary society: the health of the body at a local level, demonstrating the love of Christ for each other and for their communities, affects the health of the body on a national and international level. Worshipping communities which speak powerfully of God's saving love for his people, which empower people to take that message of hope into their workplaces and lives, and which impact local communities, will have rooted themselves in relationship with God and with one another.

The words we say, the things we do as church communities, should be clear statements of purpose to those who belong, those who explore and those who observe. As we gather around God's

14 Diarmaid MacCulloch, *Cranmer*, Yale University Press, 1996, p. 123.

word and around the Lord's Table, we do so as a community of faith and the timbre of that meeting speaks of what we believe.

How we gather shapes who we are and what we believe, both explicitly (through the actual content of songs, prayers and sermons) and implicitly (through the cultural ethos and personas).[15]

Our challenge is to ask ourselves what our gatherings say both explicitly and implicitly: are we shaping communities that are built up in faith and hope and love?

Belonging to God and to one another speaks of a future hope in the glory of the new creation, and interjects glimpses of that glory into a world searching for lasting meaning and purpose. John Zizioulas (b. 1931), who was the Eastern Orthodox Metropolitan of Pergamon, wrote: 'the Church's centre of gravity lies in the future, not in the past'.[16]

J. C. Ryle, writing on Peter's statement at the Transfiguration 'It is good to be here', suggests: 'The feelings of which Peter had a little foretaste, will then be ours in full experience. We shall all say with one heart and one voice, when we see Christ and all His saints, "It is good to be here".'[17]

Can we pray for boldness and confidence to proclaim 'How very good and pleasant it is' (Ps. 133) so that our vision of the future shapes our present and brings others in to a relationship with God?

---

15 M. Cosper, *Rhythms of Grace*, Crossway, 2013, p. 94.

16 Quoted in Paul McPartlan, *The Eucharist Makes the Church*, Eastern Christian Publications, 2006, p. 167.

17 J. C. Ryle, *Expository Thoughts: Mark*, William Hunt, 1884, p. 177, on Mark 9.4.

A2

CARING AND INCLUSIVE

As human beings we are good at dividing people up. And so it is in the Church as well. Past lack of inclusivity to those who are 'different' from us is one of the reasons that there are so many varieties of Church. What a denial of Jesus's prayer in John 17.21 that they may all be one. We do it, too, in our multiplicity of types of service. What might the Church, and its mission, look like if we started to plan in a genuinely inclusive way?

> I ask not only on behalf of these, but also on behalf of those who will believe in me through their word, that they may all be one. As you, Father, are in me and I am in you, may they also be in us, so that the world may believe that you have sent me. (John 17.20–21)

That would mean worship that shows God's love and is accessible and available to everyone who comes, regardless of age or culture. It would mean that everyone in our congregations could enter, join in, and engage with God. It need not mean that we all do the same things all the time – after all, it is accepted that children and young people have their own times together. Some people fear that making worship inclusive also means worship that is 'dumbed down' in some way, but good planning can result in worship that is easily accessed but at the same time deep in its spirituality because it depends on more than words and texts.

So inclusivity is one of the keys to mission; our lives and our worship are to demonstrate unity 'so that the world may believe' that the Father sent his Son to redeem creation. If people are made to feel valued, comfortable and welcomed, they will have a good experience of church and they might even come back. That means it is important to get it right every time, not just on occasions (such as occasional offices) when a lot of visitors are expected. It is an oft-quoted truism that we only have one chance to make a first impression. The reaction we are striving for is 'I didn't know church could be like that, it was good and I am going to come back'. Church has its own culture, and is the place where 'we' are at home – but it can be very difficult for those who are not in the know about any organisation or culture to go through the door for the first time (wondering where to sit, how to speak, how long it will last).

> If you want to know what being a stranger feels like, try going to a completely new sort of place – it might be a swimming pool, a betting shop, a gym, the place of worship of a different faith. What does it feel like, not knowing what the 'protocol' for your visit is?

Caring through being pastoral

As a Church we know that there are specific times in people's lives when pastoral care is needed. Within the resources for *Common Worship* there is a specific Pastoral Services book. In the introduction it says 'For the sake of those for whom it caters the Church and its liturgy need to embody that flexibility to adjust to different pastoral situations which is implied by being a church on the move. They also need to reflect that dependability, consistency and stability which is implied by the long history of the Church's worship, traditions and buildings.'[18]

It therefore contains a wealth of liturgy for key moments in people's experience of life and death. There are services of wholeness and healing, marriage, emergency baptisms and funerals. Within each of these services there are numerous options which enable the liturgy to be tailored to that which is most appropriate

---

18 *Common Worship Pastoral Services* [CWPS], p. 3.

for the situation and which enable people through the use of liturgy to feel held by the grace of God and cared for.

Yet having a specific book for pastoral services can send an unintentional message that other services such as daily prayer, an all-age gathering or the weekly Parish Communion service are not pastoral. However, every act of worship should be pastoral in some way, key in caring for the people who come to take part in it and reflecting something of the character of a caring God.

TO THINK ABOUT

• What does our worship reveal about the character of God?

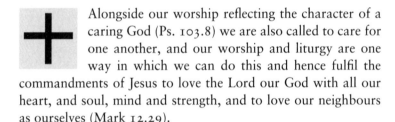 Alongside our worship reflecting the character of a caring God (Ps. 103.8) we are also called to care for one another, and our worship and liturgy are one way in which we can do this and hence fulfil the commandments of Jesus to love the Lord our God with all our heart, and soul, mind and strength, and to love our neighbours as ourselves (Mark 12.29).

Maybe the very nature of worship itself is part of long-term pastoral care, giving us the bigger perspective of God who is 'other' yet loves us, and helping us to see ourselves as loved and valued. Do we provide opportunities for both rejoicing with those who rejoice, and weeping with those who weep (Rom. 12.15)? We need to be less afraid of emotion in our worship, allowing it to be a place of joy and celebration, tears and sighing. Worship that cares enables us to bring the whole of our lives before God in worship to meet with the God who cares for the whole of our lives. We need safe space to grieve over what is going on in the world, as well as in our individual lives.

TO THINK ABOUT

• Do we provide opportunities to weep and, echoing Psalm 13, ask the big question 'How long, O Lord', in our worship?

Caring through being accessible and inclusive

If someone comes into an act of worship and is made to feel uncomfortable by other people, feels excluded or is unable to connect with the liturgy they will probably leave feeling just as they did when they entered, having received no comfort, no encouragement or challenge, and there is a high probability that they will not come back again. They may also leave with an impression of a God who stands at a distance and does not care, an impression that runs counter to our understanding of a God who is love and who runs to embrace his children. (Of course it is sometimes the Spirit who challenges people out of their comfort zones, or convicts of sin. That leads to a *good* sense of being made to feel 'uncomfortable'!)

> While he was still far off, his father saw him and was filled with compassion; he ran and put his arms around him and kissed him. (Luke 15.20)

In the Bible we are warned not to judge people, or treat them differently, because of things that are external (James 2.1–6). Yet, if we are honest with ourselves, we do it all the time and ignore (at least, until it is too late):

- people of different ages and abilities;
- people of different colours, cultures and (if we are honest!) social class;
- people with physical difficulties (such as hearing, sight or mobility issues);
- people with learning or language difficulties;
- people who learn or grow in different ways from us, which may be through listening, through action, through 'trying it out', through music or silence or images ...

TO THINK ABOUT

- What are the issues that might cause people to fall outside the boundaries that your church is happy with?

Altering the building can be expensive, but other things we can do to be inclusive are more a matter of attitude and planning than of great cost. They mean us giving thought to the way we do everything.

It would mean paying attention to the physical setting

There would be a flat space with as few changes in surface as possible; room in all parts of the building for sticks, crutches and wheelchairs; large print; a good hearing loop (how old is yours, does it work with modern hearing aids?) and/or sign language provision; accessible toilets, baby-changing facilities, warmth, light ...

> There is a church where the entrance is at the top of a steep set of stairs. A young mum visiting for the first time struggled up the steps carrying a pushchair to be met at the top by a seemingly helpful steward who said 'We have a lift you know. Oh, and the children are actually meeting in their groups this morning in the church centre at the bottom of the steps.' A weary mum made her way down the steps again ...

TO THINK ABOUT

- You might reckon your church is completely accessible to wheelchairs. But what if your president, preacher or other service leader is using crutches or a wheelchair? Inclusivity extends to them too.

A woman with profound hearing loss, who used sign language, was looking for a church. She tried several but there was no signing, no help available with following the service. Eventually she went to a church and was thrilled to discover that the whole service, including the sermon, was being signed as a matter of course. Over coffee she asked how many deaf people attended the church. 'None,' the signer told her, 'but several years ago God called me to learn to sign, and to do it every week, so that anyone who came here with profound hearing loss could take part in our worship.'

TO THINK ABOUT

• How often does your church wait until there is a need for inclusivity, rather than thinking ahead?

It would mean paying attention to the delivery of the service

Worship can be crafted beautifully, with well-chosen words and actions for the occasion, the season and the context, and yet still not connect with people if it is delivered in an unhelpful way. The most beautiful words of liturgy may be barked out by someone who sounds as if they do not care in any way for the people in front of them, or be inaudible if the microphone is not used well. The most beautiful hymn can be destroyed by an unpractised music group. If we are careless, we do little to honour the name of Jesus.

If I speak in the tongues of mortals and of angels, but do not have love, I am a noisy gong or a clanging cymbal. (1 Cor. 13.1)

There are some tips on making your voice carry in both *How to Lead the Prayers* and *How to Read the Bible in Church*.[19] People

---

19 Anna de Lange and Liz Simpson, *How to Lead the Prayers*, GBW 169, 2002; Anna de Lange and Liz Simpson, *How to Read the Bible in Church*, GBW 177, 2003.

in other jobs sometimes have training, or hints to pass on. You could ask your local theatre for help, or somebody who regularly addresses large numbers of people. If there is a sound system, use it, and make sure every person who speaks uses a microphone. People with hearing aids are relying on the technology of the T-loop, and the microphone is the pick-up.

It would mean welcoming people with different needs from our own

This entails accepting that not all parts of the worship will meet our own preferences, but will be helpful to others. If we place pastoral care in the context of worship, we can create pastoral liturgy rather than expect each service to meet 'my needs'. In turn, this enables the focus to be communal rather than individual. As the Body of Christ, as we demonstrate in word and action an awareness of the needs of one another, we reflect something of the love of God which does care for the individual. In so doing we also witness to those seeking God something of what it means to be part of the Body of Christ.

TO THINK ABOUT

- Being inclusive does not necessarily mean being all together all the time. But why should it always be the young people who go out for teaching? Could they sometimes stay in church? Or could everyone leave for appropriate activities, and come together to close the service?

 As part of their worship each week a church had a good news slot. This gave the opportunity for people to share testimonies of answers to prayer and give thanks to God, but it also gave space to value the everyday celebrations. Birthdays and anniversaries were celebrated and children who had gained certificates in school came out to share them. A young woman with additional needs would often come out to share about her most recent holiday. A memorable week involved a youngster encouraging the church to celebrate the birth of a new rabbit! This section of the service was often the part that got people talking and sharing and it demonstrated to all who came in that each person was valued – however young or old.

It would mean using a broader range of styles in our liturgy and worship

Here is another whole range of issues. We can get focused on text and (in particular) on the limits of what is and is not allowed. But is that always the best way? We could learn to worship with far fewer words by:

- increasing the amount of action;
- making greater use of symbol;
- using more pictures and images;
- giving time for imaginative use of music and silence;
- using simple words to convey complex ideas.

Of course, this all takes time – during worship as well as in preparation. (For more on putting together liturgy in different styles see A3 Creative.)

TO THINK ABOUT

- Why don't we ... (what question would you want to ask of your church worship team)?
- What could happen to our church's worship if we spent an equal amount of time on the preparation of the service itself as on the sermon?
- What effect would it have if inclusivity were a key principle in our church?

It would mean being flexible

Flexibility brings an ability to adapt quickly to different circumstances. If our worship does not recognize the complex real-life situations of people's lives it can become inaccessible and alienating. We must be able to respond when catastrophe strikes a community or an individual, and demonstrate an awareness of the context from which people are coming and a compassion for them that communicates the love of God.

TO DISCUSS

- If a service has been planned that is wall-to-wall rejoicing and then a large party arrive who have just lost a member of their family, how does your church respond?

Caring through welcoming difference

Worship that cares also does not make assumptions about the cultural background, level of faith or previous church experience of those in the congregation. Nor does it make assumptions about 'proper behaviour' or 'sufficient understanding'. These assumptions are not only made by leaders, but very often also by members of our congregations. The best welcome can be ruined in an instant by a deep sigh coming from behind. If we are truly welcoming of difference we will welcome a crying child, a bored toddler, a texting teenager, an adult with a deep and personal faith as well as learning difficulties, an old person with dementia who needs to know that they are still loved by God in spite of their confusion. A caring church guides them through the service and provides opportunities to question and explore faith. This leads us into a whole new set of implications for the way we do things.

TO THINK ABOUT

- How could our worship be changed to ensure that all are welcomed, especially those whose lifestyles mean that accessing traditional worship can be difficult?

It would mean recognizing that people have different journeys with God

It is easy to forget that all journeys are equally valid. So we might need to rethink our preconceptions and habits. How can a church reflect the demography of the area – the unemployed as well as university lecturers, various nationalities and various ages? There are some churches that are entirely mono-cultural, apparently on the (usually unspoken) basis that 'if people don't like it our way, they can go somewhere different'.

TO THINK ABOUT

- Do you know what the demography of the whole parish really is? Or are you making assumptions based on the areas round the church and the people who already attend?
- What do you think the effects of this are, both on the Christian and wider communities, and on the witness of unity?

It would mean being both multicultural and multi-linguistic

Well-planned worship accepts what others have to offer so that they can worship side by side. That implies a generosity and openness to the traditions and experiences of others. It might also involve offering an interpretation service to people who are not fluent in English, or learning to sing songs in their own mother-tongue.

TO THINK ABOUT

* Are any of your worship leaders fluent in another language? Could they offer services in that language to people in the area?

In Stratford (East London) a congregation of Bulgarian Christians hired the building of St Paul's C of E. They grew to about 60–80 people, about half living locally. In 2014 the Bulgarian language church decided to become Anglicans. Some 14 Bulgarians were baptized, 16 confirmed and 28 received into the Church of England at a service led by the Bishop of Chelmsford, Stephen Cottrell. The priest in charge of St Paul's Stratford, Revd Jeremy Fraser, has said:

> The Bulgarians have a wonderful faith. They are settled in the UK, and meet on Fridays, as they are usually working on Sunday. They are a fantastic addition to our faith community. Stratford is a place where the world comes together. Our congregation already has people who grew up around here, and people who have come here from the West Indies, from Africa, from South America and from other parts of Europe. Our pianist is Taiwanese from Canada. The kingdom of heaven will have all nations worshipping together. We feel like we are a foretaste of heaven.[20]

Caring throughout a service of worship

The challenge set before us in reimagining worship for the twenty-first century and beyond is creating worship opportunities that enable transforming encounters with the living God to take place, revealing something of his character and responding to the pastoral needs of those who gather week by week, who are all on a journey from brokenness to wholeness.

Any gathering of people for a corporate act of worship will involve individuals facing many different situations and coming

---

20 See www.chelmsford.anglican.org/news/article/East-London-church-welcomes-bulgarians-to-foretaste-of-heaven (accessed 5 November 2015).

from many different contexts. However formal or informal the worship style of a particular service, thinking through the different elements within it provides an opportunity to assess the care that people find.[21]

The greeting at the beginning of a service is crucial; it gives us the opportunity to put people at their ease; to have an idea of what is going to take place over the next hour; to help those who crawl through the door bowed down by the week to know that they are in a safe space; to enable those distracted by a thousand worries and cares to have a few moments of stillness. The right words are vital.

TO THINK ABOUT

• Does our welcome demonstrate a God who cares?

A young woman recently spoke of her experience of coming to church on Mothering Sunday. This had always been a difficult day for many reasons, yet for the first time she had not felt the odd one out that morning. The person leading the service had welcomed all those who came through the door, and acknowledged the challenge of the day for some. This had enabled her to engage with the worship, to feel supported and prayed for, and she had been able to celebrate too with those around her as children had given flowers to their mothers and others who cared for them.

The Confession is a weekly opportunity to confess sins and to hear the forgiveness of God declared. It can be the most important pastoral moment of the whole service for many; in receiving absolution and knowing the forgiveness of God they are transformed by that sense of freedom in Christ. There are many resources available for different confessions using words, symbols and music, there are many styles that can reflect the

---

21 You can find more about this, and other ideas here, in Mark Earey, *Worship that Cares*, SCM Press, 2012, especially chapter 1.

world both inside and outside the church. Having the opportunity to confess together and cry out for the mercy of God on our earth can be very powerful.

On the other hand, a balance needs to be struck. To some people worship never seems to move on from penitence. This criticism is sometimes levelled at Holy Communion services. Look through *Common Worship* Order One Communion for places where penitence is explicit: the Prayer of Preparation (otherwise known as the Collect for Purity), Prayers of Penitence, the Gloria, some of the Eucharistic Prayers, the Lord's Prayer, the Agnus Dei, the Prayer of Humble Access ... and that is before you add the singing of quiet cross-focused songs during the distribution of communion. (For more about Eucharistic worship, see C3 Eucharistic.)

TO DISCUSS

- Are we stuck in a rut, and if so might we find ways of making our forms of confession more meaningful?
- If, as is often the case, children are in church until after the confession, and return for communion, have they heard a good balance of confession, praise and thanksgiving, or does it seem that the worship is stuck in one place?

The prayers can include both intercessions for others and the offering of prayer ministry for individuals. They enable us to demonstrate God's care for the whole world and all people, and to provide a way in which we can express our care for them through the act of prayer. Yet often our prayers are rather narrow in their focus.

TO THINK ABOUT

- How often do we pray for people involved in the manufacturing industry? Does our choice of praying for councillors, teachers and doctors rather than binmen, cleaners and cooks send out an unconscious message about who is valued? (For more on intercessions, see C5 Intercessory.)

- The offering for individual prayer (whether for healing or for something else) enables us to show God's care for each person. It also empowers the body of Christ to minister to one another through the power of the Spirit.

The word of God needs to be heard and understood. It should be a matter of care to ensure that the readings are audible, and that people can find the reading if they wish to. And what if the passage is a difficult one, read with no explanation or reflection upon it? Such moments can upset and hinder people's understanding of Christianity. Moving to the sermon, or talk, does it encourage and uplift as well as challenge? Are people helped to remember the important points so that they can mull over them during the week?

The Peace can become a quick nod to the person next to you as something we have to do, or it can become a real place of reconciliation as people seek to be right with those around them before they receive communion. For some, the Peace is the only moment in their week where they receive the gift of physical touch from another human.

There was an elderly gentleman in a congregation who was a widower. As the Peace was shared with him it was the one point in his week when he had physical contact with another person. At that moment each week he knew he was part of a family and it did more for his healing than any other part of the service.

At *Communion*, in the breaking of bread and pouring out of wine, there is offered the ultimate symbol of the self-sacrificing love of God, and the knowledge of the brokenness of Christ enabling us to know wholeness. Through tangible symbols people are able to receive a reminder of God's love. For Christians this is a vital part of their worship which we do as commanded by Jesus. However, for those who are new to church it can be very confusing. In our care for those exploring faith we need to ensure that we don't put our needs before the need to reach out.

Many churches offer gluten-free bread (or wafers) to those who need it, and maybe non-alcoholic wine to those with cause not to drink alcohol. This can detract from the 'one bread, one cup' symbolism. Maybe a congregation might agree to use gluten-free bread and a non-alcoholic red drink for everyone, so as to include and support 'weaker brothers and sisters'? This might be seen as a modern-day equivalent of Paul's advice in 1 Corinthians 8 about food that had been offered to idols.

But when you thus sin against members of your family, and wound their conscience when it is weak, you sin against Christ. Therefore, if food is a cause of their falling, I will never eat meat, so that I may not cause one of them to fall. (1 Cor. 8.12–13)

TO THINK ABOUT

- Is it always appropriate to have a Communion service, especially if there will be many visitors or small children?
- How does your church help those with special dietary needs to feel included?

After-service hospitality is key in helping people to feel they belong. An invitation to share with others over a cup of coffee enables the conversations that need to be shared to happen. It allows new people to feel welcomed and to connect with others. (For more about belonging, see A1 Relational.)

But we need to think wider than this – our hospitality to those on the margins is also vital.

The Lighthouse, St George's Crypt, Leeds

The Lighthouse, a new service, was set up on a Sunday lunchtime, ministering particularly to those who (through drug and alcohol addiction) have found themselves homeless. It was designed for those for whom concentrating for longer than five minutes could be a challenge, so includes short sections with lots of practical engagement. Each service starts with a rendition of James Brown's 'You've got a friend' – a song they know and a truth they long for; this leads to an explanation of how God is the one friend that can be relied upon. There is a focus on testimony and opportunity to pray for one another. Prayer is often done in a creative way with symbols or actions to help those struggling to focus to engage. There is sensitivity to the significant proportion of people who are illiterate by using simple call-and-response liturgy. Psalms of lament are used regularly in a context where many are in great distress. Praying for one another enables the sense of community to build, and many have experienced significant encounters with God.[22]

TO THINK ABOUT

• Would someone who came from the margins of society feel welcomed and be able to access your act of worship?

The whole structure of the service as well as its individual elements is vitally important – especially its length. You can have many, many very pastorally appropriate and caring aspects to a service, but if there are too many elements which cause the service to go on for over two hours (when people were not expecting this to be the case) it can cause discomfort, and despair among the children's group leaders if the church is fortunate to have them, and exhaustion among parents if it isn't.

22 For more information, see www.stgeorgescrypt.org.uk/charity/ component/k2/item/362-the-lighthouse-family.html (accessed 25 August 2016).

Some things to consider in your context

- Being caring and accessible does not necessarily equate with comprehensibility – the parables are very accessible, but not always easy to understand. You can use simple language to convey complex ideas.
- Comfort is not just physical (though that helps!); in order to feel at ease people also need to understand the shape and length of the liturgy. The use of projection often gives no sense of that. You could print a service outline on the notice-sheet, or use a progress bar along the bottom of the screen to counteract this.
- When they produce printed material some churches seem intent on getting as many words on a page as they can. Legibility guidelines recommend an absolute minimum size of well-spaced 12-point Arial for clear text, and anything described as large print should be at least 16-point Arial.[23]
- Use images and language that relate to your community and congregation, which might mean reimagining some of the fishing and shepherding language of the Bible in order to make it speak.
- Personality and leading skills are key to helping the liturgy speak for itself; some leaders are better than others at giving sufficient explanation at key points of the service without sounding patronizing.
- There can be a considerable difference between the styles you use for leader texts (where language can be more complex) and congregational texts (where language needs to be simpler, with short sentences). This is something to watch out for when you use imported services or materials from other organizations, even other churches of your denomination, as the balance is not always right.

---

23 For more help on this look for 'clear print guidelines' on any internet search engine. Leaflets and guidance are downloadable from the websites of organizations such as the RNIB and UKAAF (UK Association for Accessible Formats).

TO DISCUSS

Take some time to think about caring and inclusivity in relation to other chapters in this book. What difference would it make to your approach to (for instance) preaching, or Holy Communion, or funerals?

A3

CREATIVE

A creative God

If our attitudes to caring and accessibility are going to be carried through into our worship, it almost certainly follows that the way we do things will change.

We see from the biblical record that God is God of the ever-present – 'I am who I am' – and ever-changing in his ways of communicating with his people. But are humans able to be 'tense-less' as God is? We are bound in space and time, as God is not, and in order to 'keep up' with him, we need to be able to change, reform, be renewed. We see God moving in new ways, Jesus bringing a new kingdom; we see in scripture various encouragements to us to keep moving and changing.

> Sing to him **a new song**; play skilfully on the strings, with loud shouts. (Ps. 33.3)
>
> ... and they **sing a new song** before the throne. (Rev. 14.3)
>
> So if anyone is in Christ, there is a **new creation**. (2 Cor. 5.17)
>
> I am about to do a **new thing**: now it springs forth, do you not perceive it? (Is. 43.19)
>
> When you send forth your spirit, they are created; and you **renew** the face of the ground. (Ps. 104.30)

Moreover, Jesus was constantly challenging the 'norm' and the traditional. He spoke to a Samaritan woman, he touched a leper, he stilled a storm, he gave old teachings new interpretations

CREATIVE

(Matt. 5.44, Love your enemies ...). Living with Jesus must have been a continual series of surprises and, in the end, his disciples learnt from him, so that they battled through their preconceived ideas to spread the gospel to the Gentiles and to form a church made up of every conceivable type of person. Paul, writing to the Colossians, could say: 'for in him all things in heaven and on earth were created, things visible and invisible, whether thrones or dominions or rulers or powers, all things have been created through him and for him. He himself is before all things, and in him all things hold together' (Col. 1.16–17).

Following a Lord who not only had authority over the laws of nature, but who actually created them, must have encouraged the disciples to believe that anything was possible, not least the re-creation of the human heart. The way they gathered together reflected this, both in practice (mixing slaves and free, Jews and Gentiles), and in their worship, where everyone was able to take part.

Re-creating caring worship

In very many ways *Common Worship* is supportive of inclusivity. It has outline services for most types of service, allowing leaders to construct their own liturgies (spoken and unspoken) with very few constraints. In addition, the rubrics and the Notes are very carefully constructed to show points in a printed liturgy where flexibility is especially appropriate. 'The president may use these or other words' (see, for instance, the introduction to the baptism service). If you deconstruct these words they mean that you don't have to use this part of the service at all, and if you do you can use any suitable words. In essence it says, 'Something like this is a good idea here'.[24]

When we look slightly beyond the main volume, which was of necessity focused on text, the width of what is permitted (even encouraged) in worship becomes more apparent. The chapters

---

24 You can find the baptism service in CWPS p. 349, or *Common Worship Christian Initiation* [CWCI], p. 63.

that come before the resource sections in NPW give a great deal of advice and stimulus, not least in the 'stories of the four churches'. Yet many people skip over these chapters in their rush to find a good text for the next service.

While there is flexibility in *Common Worship*, in a lot of circumstances it is not enough, and is often hard to find as well. Why are there so many instances where the permitted variations may not become the normal on a Sunday? Where are the permissions and helpful guidelines, for example, for the café church wanting to have worship which includes baptism, or communion?

Sometimes it seems, to those at the outposts of the Church, that those in the centre don't quite understand what it's like on the fuzzy fringes, and that they still don't go far enough in providing liturgy which those on the way to faith in Christ can feel comfortable using.

With the best will in the world a book of words is not a good vehicle for conveying the importance of symbolism, action and silence. We need to see or experience non-verbal worship as it cannot be adequately described. Moreover, any text that is put together to be printed for wide use tends to require a higher reading age than the more informal spoken word. Sometimes we need more freedom to paraphrase what is printed, to put it into our own words, so that it suits the congregation in front of us.

Perhaps we are moving to an age where, with 'christendom' no longer having any meaning, and most people not being familiar with any kind of liturgical language, we need to be brave enough to drop some of our 'authorized' texts, or at least keep the number as few as is feasible. The language, pictures and symbolism used in the creed or in some baptismal texts seem unintelligible to all but a very small minority.

Why do people need to be taught a great amount of biblical history, background and narrative before worshipping the God who is ever-changing? Why is their everyday language not good enough? Many studies of inculturation have shown the difference worshipping in one's own language makes to faith, but we don't seem to be able to put it into practice in most English churches!

Anyone who has tried to explain the Nicene Creed or the creedal baptismal affirmations to children or interested adults who have not been brought up within the church, will be aware of how difficult it is. Even many intelligent Christians who don't have a theological education find the eucharistic prayers difficult. Do we need to accept that packing so much doctrine into our liturgy every week is not the best way for people to grow in their faith?

We may consider that church governance is boring, but unless those voices are heard at regional and national levels the demand for flexibility goes unexpressed. Those who want change and open structures need to engage with councils and synods.[25]

TO THINK ABOUT

• Could God be calling you (or someone you know) to stand for election to a governing body within the wider Church?

FOR THE WIDER CHURCH

• As we look to the future we need to think about the challenge of incorporating flexibility into worship books that are of necessity word-based and linear.
• How might we extend the principles of NPW even further, while maintaining a family likeness within our services?
• Could we work out more outline services with different structures?
• How might we produce resource sections which include instructions for acted-out liturgy?

---

25 For more on where the flexibility could be increased, see Mark Earey, *Beyond Common Worship*, SCM Press, 2013; or Ian Tarrant, *Worship and Freedom in the Church of England*, GBW 210, 2012.

A creative church

As human beings we frequently hang on to the familiar and resist change. We do it in all sorts of ways – in our daily routines, our favourite foods, our shopping and, not least, in our churches. What has worked for us in the past is what will work again ... After centuries of worship 'by the book' how can we rediscover our God-given and Spirit-inspired creativity?

TO THINK ABOUT

- Does renewal inevitably bring change? Does it equal creativity?
- What does the ever-present God who is 'I am who I am' desire from us as we worship?

The changing assumptions of a new generation of Christians

We have now gone past Gen X and Y, but we can all see that the needs of different generations are very different from our own. It is easy to say 'When I was young ...' and expect today's youngsters to be the same, but that never works. Why should it? There may be nothing wrong with a younger generation's attitude, except that it is different from our own. Different is not always worse, it can be better. For example, the generation brought up on events such as Soul Survivor take it as a matter of course that there will be frequent occasions when they pray together, in groups of friends. Their informality means that it is very easy for them to move from talking together, to praying for each other, and back again.

TO THINK ABOUT

- What could your church learn from the younger (or older!) people in the congregation?

Changing understandings as we journey together

Our theology and practice is not immutable and sometimes needs to change. For example, the majority of Christians no longer believe that slavery is acceptable, or that women should not be in leadership positions over men. And our theological understanding should be reflected in our practice, in our daily life and also in our worship. We need to reconnect the way we live our lives and the way we create our worship.

TO THINK ABOUT

• What do we take for granted in daily life, but neglect to recognize in our worship?

New stages of life

We have grown used to worshipping together in the same way, and to church members fitting in to what the church is doing. But sometimes we need to turn that on its head and fit in with what people are doing. For example, we are familiar with theories of human growth and development but may not let them affect our church structures, apart from special activities for children. Perhaps we need to do some thinking about the ways in which new life stages affect the way we relate to church. For example, can God still do a new thing when a person retires? And if so, how do we celebrate / confirm / teach that through our liturgy? How does God work through the teenager who has just passed his or her driving test, or the older person who has just retired? (See D2 Crossing Thresholds.)

TO THINK ABOUT

• Do the worship leaders and preachers in the church you attend all come from one similar group of people? Could the responsibility be shared more widely?

Expressing creativity

If liturgy needs art, architecture and music to express the un-spoken, then creativity is necessary in order to interpret liturgy for a new generation. But we may need to think about who is being creative – is it just the leadership, or is the whole con-gregation, of every age, encouraged to be creative in the way that they worship together?

TO THINK ABOUT

- In our worship we are often good at encouraging musicians; but what about artists, potters, cooks, writers, embroiderers or woodturners?

Fresh Expressions of church are trying out various ways of all this, in different contexts, and seem to be an easier way to access the church for many people. Both in mission and in disciple-ship it makes sense to meet people where they are, whether that be through arts and craft, love of nature, music or in different age groups. The success of Messy Church in many different contexts is because although there is a fixed 'menu' of what can be offered, which is based on play, crafts, food and accessible worship, it can also be translated into groups which reach out to others through sports, music and nature-based activity.[26]

TO THINK ABOUT

- Could you visit a local 'Fresh Expression' to experience their creativity, and see if anything would transfer to your context (even in a small way)?

---

26 For more about Fresh Expressions, see Matt Stone, *Fresh Expres-sions of Church*, GBEv 92, 2010; and Tim Sumpter, *Freshly Expressed Church*, GBEv 109, 2015. Messy Church can be found at www.messy church.org.uk.

TO DISCUSS

• Would changing the way your church normally does (for example) the sermon, or the prayers, mean that a wider range of people could be involved? How would you go about that?

How can we keep familiarity as well as freshness?

If our texts are fixed and unchanging, they do not adapt to new realities in the lives of the world, the Church and the people. On the other hand, if we have no fixed texts (or even no texts at all) we can be equally captive to either the past ('the way we've always done it') or the ever-changing immediate context.

We are human and need some structure in our lives, so it is important not to completely throw out the old. Many people find comfort in familiarity, and the tenacity of, for example, BCP services in the countryside and in nursing homes bears witness to this, as do the requests for baptism (or rather, christening!) – on a Sunday, in a familiar church building, with traditional 'churchy' things like a robed vicar and hymns sung to organ accompaniment.

But there is a balance to be sought, as even those congregations appreciate informality, a chance to participate, and building relationships together. The original *Patterns for Worship* (in 1995), and then *Common Worship*, with their 'directory' approach, enabled this to take place in a way which can use the familiar service structures and words while at the same time include new and creative elements.

> We have a faithful but elderly congregation for the 8 a.m. BCP Holy Communion service. They have always arrived, attended the service, and left again. But a few months ago we introduced 'tea and toast', just one Sunday a month. People have told us that they had been coming to church with the same people for years, but had never spoken to them (or in some cases even known their names). The whole atmosphere, every week, has changed and there is now a buzz and a sense of community. What's more, the numbers are going up!

At the same time there is always a need to keep asking if our creativity is only aimed at entertainment, or whether it is, as it should be, aimed at formation. Perhaps the best way to tell is by the fruits shown in people's lives – those who are used to being entertained are most likely to have a 'pew fodder' mentality and approach worship in a judgemental way – does this service appeal to my personality and spirituality? This is in contrast to people growing in faith and in confidence that they have something to offer others.

> A life-time churchgoer said that the sermon used to be the most boring part of the service; now she looks forward to it so that she can understand more of the scriptures and hear God speaking to her.

There are, of course, some things in which choice is limited and we need to stick to the authorized texts, for example, with the Creeds and Authorized Affirmations of Faith. The reason that we are limited has to do with doctrine, and what the church believes. Even so, this can feel awkward in the context of a service where many of those attending are not regular churchgoers, or who are at the beginning of a faith journey. These circumstances should lead us into deeper thought about why we use a common liturgy, and what principles would guide us in using something different.

TO DISCUSS

• Are there things in your regular liturgy that some people experience as an obstacle? Have you ever asked them what they find difficult? Do you need to change? Do you need to explain things more, or better?

Creativity in practice

Service structures

The very style in which *Common Worship* books are put together encourages creativity in planning and leading services. There is a structure page at the beginning of nearly all the groups of services which, if followed, keeps the order of each one broadly the same and provides some familiarity or 'family likeness' in the service. But within this structure, a huge range of ways to use items in the service is possible. The notes at the beginning and end of the service also encourage the use of a variety of ways of treating each of the elements of the service. For example, in the Structure of a Service of the Word there is the heading 'Proclaim and respond to the word of God'. The proclamation might mean a sermon, but the proclamation and response might just as easily include things like arts and crafts, discussion, silence, song-writing or poetry, involving not just the leader but several people or the whole congregation – gathered together or in smaller groups, in one location or several. NPW not only provides resources for the different parts of the service, but also has some guidance on personalizing them for local contexts and on writing your own.[27]

Team building

Try to grow your worship-leading team. The picture we get of ministry in the New Testament is of a group of leaders together, and of different people taking a part in leadership and in worship. The idea of 'collaborative ministry' is gradually taking root in the Church of England too, although many people, non-churchgoers and regulars, still seem to think that the church can't function without the vicar. But it is imperative that more than one person is involved in planning and leading worship, for all sorts of reasons, not least that more people means more ideas, more creativity and more resources. If we are to engage people of different gender, background and personality type in worship, we need a range of

---

27 There are creative ideas for the 'sermon slot' in Anna de Lange, *How to Engage with Scripture*, GBW 207, 2011.

leaders who can connect with all these different factors. For example, if most clergy are introverts, churches need some extroverts on the leadership team too, and the same applies to those who express themselves best in words, or music, art or sculpture.[28]

Authenticity

Try to be true to the people you are. Some people in the Anglican church seem to have a 'one size fits all' view of worship, which means in practice that many churches try to emulate cathedrals or other models. What if we got it into our heads that we're all different, and that God would love us to worship him with integrity? That might mean that a small congregation of unmusical people decide to stop singing hymns to the backing of CDs, and enjoy worship without the stress of having to sing. Or a parish might decide to do some re-ordering of their church so that there are more windows through which they can see the glory of creation inspiring their worship. Or a group could go running together after they've met for Bible study and prayer, expressing their response to God physically. One of the values of the Fresh Expressions movement is that it helps us to see that God can be worshipped in many different ways, and that traditional church is not always what will help unchurched people best.

> As an example, we could take the resources for Advent in CWTS. There are churches which have the resources to run a service with a splendid choir, using flexible lighting, the patterns of readings suggested and some evocative poetry. There are others which have none of these things, where a Christmas Bazaar is held in the afternoon on Advent Sunday, followed by a short time of prayers and a reflection setting the tone for the run-up to Christmas. A Messy Church meeting near the beginning of Advent might use the theme of light and darkness to make all sorts of crafts, and produce an Advent Ring to be used in the worship at any weekly service in Advent.

---

28 For more on building a team to lead worship, see Trevor Lloyd and Anna de Lange, *How to Share the Leadership of Worship*, GBW 199, 2009.

Words and meaning

Try to cut the jargon. Sometimes we may be restric-
tive, and keeping people from joining us, by our basic
language. What do people understand by 'service'
and 'worship'? (Clue – think what they see on TV!)
Many churches have found that meeting café-style and using a
name such as 'Sunday@ten' is both more attractive, and means
that non-regulars can join in because they are no longer required
to fit in with churchgoing traditions like hymns and sermons.
Given good coffee and encouraged to chat to neighbours and
friends, people are happy to participate and share faith in a way
they wouldn't be willing to do in a formal service structure.

Locations

Try holding services out of the church building. It is easy to
interpret the service structures in *Common Worship* as being
intended for a traditional church service on a Sunday, but there
is no reason why worship cannot take place in another location,
a community hall, a home, or outdoors. There are many reasons
why a congregation may have to move out of their church
temporarily, and they often find that a different space makes
them look at worship in a new way. So why not occasionally
move out of church into the town centre, or the local park, or a
farmer's barn, and experiment with how worship might be different in unusual surroundings. Could the way we use creation
psalms change if we can see the sky above us and grass beneath
our feet? Do our prayers include different people if we pray them
in the middle of a street of shops? Might our view of the con-
tribution of children to our worship change when we meet in
their school hall? (See A4 Located.)

The 'best'?

It can be salutary to think about who we choose to be 'allowed'
to contribute, and whose gifts we value. Some take the line that
'only the best is good enough for God' – but whose 'best' do we

mean? For centuries, our churches have been enhanced by beautiful architecture, art and music, but should that prevent others from offering their best to God? Isn't the altar-frontal made by the children's group as honouring to God as the one made by a professional needlewoman? Isn't the Advent ring made by the café-church congregation as beautiful in God's eyes as the one made by a member of the regular flower-arranging team?

Often, and not only in the countryside, local people who don't normally attend church give their time and money to maintaining or repairing the church's bricks and mortar, or the churchyard. They see what they are doing as 'my bit' for God or the church. Might we find ways of not only valuing what they do, but using it as a bridge to come nearer to the God they reach out tentatively for, by finding ways of worship which do not involve the traditional church structures?

A4

LOCATED

'By her relationship with Christ, the Church is a kind of sacrament or sign of intimate union with God and of the unity of all mankind. She is also an instrument for the achievement of such union and unity.'[29]

Just as the above is true for the Church as the people of God, so it is also true for the building in which God's people meet. Church spaces are about more than just the functions that take place within them. They have in their very design a significance declaring who and what matters, what the values of the church are and what that says about the God we worship. When there is failure to meet the needs of particular groups, when the past is idealized and used to resist change, when we believe that our generation has nothing to add today to the heritage of tomorrow, we send the wrong messages to the world that God loves and we misrepresent the Christian faith.

TO THINK ABOUT

Take a critical look at the church building where you worship.

- What does it say about God?
- What does it say about the church's values?
- And about who you are in relationship to both God and the church?

---

29 Second Vatican Council, *Dogmatic Constitution on the Church*, *Number 1*.

What is the church building for?

How you arrange and use your worship space will depend to a considerable extent on your theology of the purpose of the building. This varies from church to church, and to some extent with time.

In a seminal work Harold W. Turner (1911–2002) attempts to examine the place of sacred buildings, and he distinguishes between the 'domus dei' or Temple and the 'domus ecclesia' or Meeting House as locations for the presence of God. In the 'house of God' he can be met through sacred rites and actions; these are mediated through the priesthood, and there is a hierarchy not just of human rank but also of liturgical space. However, in the 'house of the church', as in the Synagogue, it is the teacher who leads the people as it were 'in the round', and the presence of God is perceived in the fellowship with one another.[30]

Howard Marshall takes this thought further in an examination of what role, if any, the Jewish Temple had in the worship of the early Church, concluding that first of all Jesus, and then the gathered believers, replaced the need for a specific building.[31]

God is present when we gather in three ways: first because his presence pervades the universe; second because Jesus is present in each of the believers individually, and third because there is a particular presence in the gathered community (reflecting the Rabbinic insight that when two gather to study the Law the Shekinah or glory of God is present – Pirque Aboth 3.3).

Spiritualization is the idea that a religious rite without the correct attitude of heart is worthless, and also therefore that you can dispense with the rite altogether if your heart is in the right place. The Jews had this forced on them with the destruction of the Jerusalem Temple, but Jesus in the Gospels seems to be saying that the new Temple was his body. Furthermore, in the book of Revelation we find that the heavenly city had no need of a Temple because of the presence of the Lord God and the Lamb.

---

30 H. W. Turner, *From Temple to Meeting House*, Mouton, 1979.
31 I. H. Marshall, 'Church and Temple in the New Testament', *Tyndale Bulletin* 40.2, 1989, pp. 203–22

I saw no temple in the city, for the temple is the Lord God the Almighty and the Lamb. (Rev. 21.22)

Christian places of worship today vary enormously between the extremes of temple or a meeting house. Your building may not say what you want about the kind of God you worship. If all the seats face the front and all the action happens there, people might, over time, get an idea that God is distant, separate from them – and that worship is largely about observing rather than participating. If you can have a circle of people sitting around tables, it might send out different signals about what God is like. However, you may have a building you cannot change much. Perhaps you can compensate by the manner in which you worship, or in other areas of church life.

TO THINK ABOUT

- Do the people see your church building as temple or meeting house? What implications does this have for what they want of the building?
- Is your building, and its furniture, flexible enough to serve as both temple and meeting house?

Changes to buildings in the *Common Worship* era

Some thought that *Common Worship*, in which practically every service has a eucharistic shape, would further increase the centrality of Holy Communion as the primary act of Anglican worship. Its rich provision of liturgical material would resource the journey along an already well-established trajectory. Consequently changes in church architecture would follow an established pattern: the communion table brought west of the screen or down into the body of the church and positioned more centrally, choir positioned behind the communion table and the congregation gathered round the other three sides. Such changes are evidenced in numbers of church reorderings or rebuilds.

Examples include the rebuilt St Barnabas', Dulwich Village, St Brandon's, Brancepeth (Co. Durham) which was gutted by fire in 1998, or the hexagonal church of St Luke, Buckfastleigh, with central table and font, built to replace the old parish church of Holy Trinity on the hill outside the town when that was burnt down.

Although such changes have indeed taken place since *Common Worship* was published, there are other liturgical and cultural changes that are having a far greater impact on church spaces. These changes are impacting both worship areas and ancillary spaces.

Worship areas

> It was probably the buzz of conversation before and after the 8.00 a.m. communion that alerted us to the change, but it could have been the way that when it was *Common Worship* rather than BCP everyone shared the Peace with everyone else, or that when we gave the congregation the choice of sitting dispersed on pews across the nave or seated together in the carpeted and chaired chapel, the chapel was chosen.

Something similar to this comment has brought a change in today's churchgoers and it is impacting on both the layout of the worship space and in the ancillary spaces churches need. Fifty years ago if a person was involved in church, attending church was something you did for an hour on Sunday before going to the pub or coming home for Sunday lunch. Today if you are involved in church you are more likely to say you *belong* to a church, that church is something you are part of. This transition from those who attend to those who belong is one of the key drivers of the changes that are taking place. The needs of attenders are very different from the needs of belongers. Church buildings are consequently being restructured as a result of the transition from one sort of church affiliation to another. We will go on to explore how a belonging church needs different spaces to an attending church later, but first we need to identify one of the biggest changes affecting internal church layout.

Projection and other technology

Common Worship could be described as the definitive work of the printed word liturgical family and it is the digitally projected image that has done most to challenge its liturgical dominance and altered the architecture of church spaces. Where once the DAC.[32] called for worship advice from those with expertise in church organs, now it is the audio-visual specialist who is called upon to guide the parish with the where, what and how of fitting screens and projectors or positioning the 24-channel mixing desk and camera controls. The rise in the numbers of worshippers attending services led by music/worship groups and the continued decline in the number of robed choirs and associated congregations has become a self-perpetuating driver of further change.

The advantages of using a screen rather than printed words are multiple.

- It does away with the heap of books and papers handed out at the door and enables the ministry of greeting and welcoming to be exactly that.
- It encourages singing by lifting heads and voices.
- It is good for parents juggling children, and for those who are new to church and unfamiliar with the service.
- It enables the service leader to act as a 'gatherer', pulling together liturgical material from wide-ranging sources.
- It enables the latest songs to move seamlessly from their first airing at the New Wine conference to the following Sunday morning worship.
- The notices that are on the loop before and after the service can move smoothly to website and social media pages.

---

32 The Diocesan Advisory Committee for the Care of Churches, including a variety of experts and representatives of amenity societies, advises church leaders about anything they want to do to their buildings, as well as the senior legal official of the diocese, the Chancellor. See the website of the Cathedral and Church Buildings Division of the Archbishops' Council, http://www.churchcare.co.uk

- It can transform the sermon not simply with business style presentations, but by opening up the possibility for inclusion of film clips of every type, cartoons or even live projection of a larger-than-life preacher.

However, in our enthusiasm to embrace the technology, we need to beware of drawbacks, which are sometimes not apparent for a while:

- seating has always to face a screen (at least, until church chairs are available with an airline-style screen in the chair-back in front!) and that can prevent more interesting and community-building layouts;
- the focus is on the screen, rather than on the service-leader or the action;
- there is often no clue of where in the service we are: how does a visitor know whether this is a 30-minute service that is nearly over, or a two-hour one that has only just begun?
- hymns and prayers are screened in bite-sized chunks, making it hard to think about the words in advance;
- it often becomes impossible for those who arrive early to think and pray through the service before it starts;
- increased flexibility often leads to less stability, and fewer liturgical texts become known by heart;
- if the screen starts to govern sermon preparation, depth and teaching can become less important than visual impact.[33]

It is not just Sunday worship that has been dramatically altered, for digital imagery has also (by public request) become part of the pastoral offices. There are increasing numbers of funerals where families ask 'Can we show a photo montage accompanied by his favourite songs?' Similarly some weddings do away with the expense or inconvenience of orders of service and have all the congregation's words projected; others choose a narrative in pictures of the couple's journey to their wedding day that provides backing pictures to the service liturgy.

33 For more on projection, see Ian Tarrant, *How to Worship with Data Projection*, GBW 192, 2007.

All-age and family services have been transformed but this technology is not necessarily going to stop here – and could become divisive in ways we have not yet seen. In 50 years (or even 15) might we be sending the service to everyone's mini-device or tablet? Would that mean you didn't even need to attend church, but could log-in at a distance?

Layout and liturgy

There are other important influences on how the worship areas are arranged and used. Not the least of these is the liturgy itself, which makes demands on various elements of the building. To take just a few examples:

- for a Eucharist you need good sightlines so that the congregation can see as well as hear the action;
- for baptism you need gathering space with room for lots of water and a floor that can get wet without damage;
- for congregational participation you need space for moving around;
- for even a modest music group you need space for music stands, microphones, possibly a keyboard or a drumkit.

A number of issues arise when a church begins to address the issues raised by the traditional 'pew and pulpit' arrangement of worship areas. There is a labyrinthine path to follow through the workings of Listed Building Consent, municipal planning offices, heritage bodies and (for Church of England buildings) Faculty Jurisdiction. That is quite apart from the natural conservatism of many in our congregations and wider parishes. Some ideas and examples of what can be done are to be found in books or, better, by visiting other churches in your area which have already made changes.[34]

---

34 For example, see Richard Giles, *Repitching the Tent*, Canterbury Press, 1996.

TO THINK ABOUT

Does what you would like to do to your worship area sit well
with the answer to the first question in this section, about
temple vs meeting house? Is the balance right?

Buildings and mission

The traditional facilities that church buildings have offered,
often simply a clergy and a choir vestry (maybe with a tap in the
churchyard!) fall short of the needs of a congregation that is a
living community.

Welcome and social needs

The journey to faith often starts with belonging, and
an important part of church life is developing friend-
ships, as demonstrated by the congregation chatter
at the 8.00 a.m. Communion above. At its most
basic, today's building needs a place for before- and after-service
chat with a cup of coffee or juice. Innovative and creative ways
are being found to add kitchen facilities to even the smallest rural
church. Flexible spaces may be created by the removal of pews at
the back or in a side aisle, with a 'kitchen in a cupboard' added
in one corner.

But the most basic and essential of these facilities is toilets:
having good toilets is the most fundamental need for any civilized
modern building.

There are many reasons why toilets are more essential than
they were. Congregations include a much wider age range than
in earlier eras with represen-
tation from the very young to
the very old. Holy Communion
is a longer service than Matins,
especially with a decent length
of sermon, intercessions led by
a member of the congregation

When one church sought planning
permission for toilets, the council's
building conservation officer
asked if congregations were more
incontinent than they used to be!

and a healthy number of communicants. The service can last an hour and a half (or longer) and those who attend may have a significant journey to and from home. Similarly, more informal services of the word, with extended times of praise and intimate worship as well as teaching and ministry, can last for comparable lengths of time.

Those who *belong* to church want to stay to talk to friends, find out information about activities and events or just enjoy the after-service refreshments. Gone are the days when people attended their nearest church: nowadays 15 minutes' travel to church is not unusual. Were such a family to arrive five minutes before a service that lasts an hour and a half, stay afterwards for 30 minutes for refreshments and then travel 15 minutes home, they have been out for two and a half hours. That is a length of time in which a significant number of people would need toilet facilities. Curiously, if they came only once a month they might be spending more time in church than a member of the Matins congregation who attended weekly.

Belonging is not just about adults; churches have invested heavily in youth and children's workers and family ministry. Those churches who have worked hard to gain or retain children and young people will want to ensure that there are adequate facilities to meet their needs.

A building which is not just for worship

There is a holistic strength and theological truth in the interconnectedness of worship, fellowship, learning and life. That the place where baptism preparation happens is the place of baptism, that the wedding surgery is the other side of the door to where couples will stand and make eternal promises, that coffee is shared under the same roof where bread and wine are shared. The mum who comes with her child to a toddler class knows what to expect when she comes to pram service. The dad who brings his lad to youth club knows where the men's prayer breakfast will be. The lady from afternoon sewing knows where Wednesday Communion will be and the friends she will see again there. God in Christ is drawing all things back to himself. Christianity declares that the gnosticism of today is as false as it always was, that secular and sacred cannot be divided. That the arms of Jesus are fully God and fully Man.

Mission changes worship, changes buildings

A drowning man learns to swim quickly. The arrival of more missional worship acts as a driver to change the church building including the desire to adapt it to be more flexible. The desire to create open spaces or to exchange pews for moveable furniture grows out of the development of new forms of worship: Messy Church, café church, youth and alternative worship, Celtic or Taizé-style services, there is a growing variety of new and innovative mission-orientated services shaped by the local context.

Church growth studies have identified eight characteristics of growing churches:

- planting new congregations and Fresh Expressions;
- making worship less stiff, more relaxed and varied;
- better provision for children and young people;
- improving welcome and integration;
- better quality, more varied, contemporary music;
- more lay involvement in leadership;
- better small groups and pastoral care;
- improvements to buildings.

As we reflect on these, it becomes apparent that all to a greater or lesser extent have an impact on the church building. The simple growth-focused decision of having an additional morning service of a different style requires either a gap of time or space for those wanting to socialize afterwards; more relaxed worship changes the shape; good provision for children means a place where they can learn appropriately.

Costly giving

The changes made to church buildings are not cheap, and it is congregational sacrificial giving that practically always has to cover the cost. This can only happen if the worship has so nurtured and strengthened faith and commitment to Christ that congregation members will give of their time, their skills and their money to create churches that are better for mission, that meet the needs of the community they serve and that glorify God. That growth in faith and commitment has been achieved for many through the weekly diet of *Common Worship* services that has nourished and nurtured them.

TO THINK ABOUT

- List all the ways in which your church building is used, both week by week and throughout the year.
- What are you asking of the spaces that you have?
- Dream some dreams about what you could achieve if some of those spaces were to change.

A5

WELL-LED

Some person, or a small group of people, needs to have responsibility for having a vision for the worship of a church. Where is it going, how might it develop, and how will it get there? Maybe there will be the vision of a congregation together in worship, led on each occasion by the word and the Spirit, and steered by a leader. Within each act of worship there will be different parts to be facilitated by the leader or leaders, and the gathering of the people together into a worshipping community is a crucial role. Theologically it is God who gathers us, but in practice that act of gathering is mediated (as are all the other aspects of our corporate worship) through human beings.

In recent decades there has been a shift in perception of the role of the worship leader, reflected in the move from calling the person 'in charge' the officiant or the celebrant, to referring to the president, presider or presiding minister.

The terminology of 'president' is found in Justin Martyr's accounts of worship in Rome in the mid-second century, and has now become a dominant term across many different denominations, particularly in relation to the Eucharist. We do not know whether Justin uses the term in his accounts because it was regularly used in Christian worship in many places, or because it was peculiar to worship at Rome, or because it was a term that his audience would understand, but which was not actually in use in the church.

From terminology to practice

This shift in terminology reflects a shift in understanding about the role of the worship leader. It moves from a model which suggests the leader is the person 'doing' the worship, which can push the congregation into a supporting, or even observing, role, to a model in which the congregation are the chief 'do-ers' of worship, with the presider acting like the chair of a meeting, overseeing the process and making sure that everyone can play their part.

In the Church of England, the bishop is seen as the senior 'presider' for the diocese, from whom presiding at local services is delegated. Presiding over the church's worship is seen as reflecting and deriving from a wider role in presiding over other aspects of the church's life: overseeing pastoral care, teaching, mission, and so on. At local church level, the same is true.

From the *Common Worship* service for the Ordination and Consecration of a Bishop

'Obedient to the call of Christ and in the power of the Holy Spirit, [bishops] are to gather God's people and celebrate with them the sacraments of the new covenant.'
From the Introduction

'As principal ministers of word and sacrament, stewards of the mysteries of God, [bishops] are to preside at the Lord's table and to lead the offering of prayer and praise ...

'They are to baptize and confirm, nurturing God's people in the life of the Spirit and leading them in the way of holiness. They are to discern and foster the gifts of the Spirit in all who follow Christ, commissioning them to minister in his name. They are to preside over the ordination of deacons and priests, and join together in the ordination of bishops.

> 'As chief pastors, it is their duty to share with their fellow presbyters the oversight of the Church, speaking in the name of God and expounding the gospel of salvation.'
> *From the Declarations*

Parish priests preside (by default) because of their role in the church community, so that their liturgical role reflects and reinforces their pastoral role.

Of course, others share in leadership of worship too. This includes Readers (Licensed Lay Ministers, as they are called in some dioceses) and in some dioceses this extends to others who are given a bishop's licence for particular leadership and ministry roles. This is part of that same model of worship leadership being 'under authority' from the bishop and, with that, a sense that it needs to be accountable beyond the local church. Before the bishop will give a licence, there is usually a need for some sort of training for the role which is to be taken up.

TO THINK ABOUT

In the church you go to:

- Who has responsibility for the overall picture of worship?
- Who makes sure that every act of worship is planned, or allocates it to a particular person?
- Who makes sure that everything happens as it should?
- If this is done by one person, could the responsibilities be shared? And who might be on the group?

A good leader?

So what are the qualities that we should be looking for, in trying to discern who might be asked to lead worship, and to undertake training for the role? There are many roles in worship that can nurture these qualities, such as reading the Bible passages, leading intercessions, or conducting interviews. It becomes apparent if someone has a gift for such a ministry. We should be on the alert for people who are:

- open to the leading of God's Spirit, and alert to the needs and responses of the congregation;
- aware of how the whole service hangs together, though not expected to explain its rationale at every opportunity;
- able to pass the baton to different contributors, verbally, by gesture, or just by eye contact;
- ready to spot newcomers and help them with a little more information, without their feeling singled out. 'We'll be reading the Psalm from the green prayer book ...' (so not the blue hymn book, and not the brown Bible);
- flexible enough to make minor changes to the service plan ('After that sermon let's take a few moments to reflect quietly, instead of singing the hymn'), but wise enough to do so without discarding somebody else's preparation or practice;
- responsive to unforeseen occurrences: 'The Wardens have just carried out somebody who fainted in the back row – let's pray for her ...';
- able to command the attention and confidence of the congregation. In a different context we might call this 'having stage presence'.

Accountability?

Of course, much leadership of worship does not have that wider sense of connectedness and accountability that comes with being an authorized minister. This has always been true of musical leaders, whether organists, choir leaders, music group or worship band leaders. However, *Common Worship* encourages a wider sharing, extending to others who regularly preach or lead worship (or share in leading worship – for instance a small group who take responsibility for a monthly all-age service) without a licence from the bishop.

If those who are to take part are to lead people to God, discernment and training will be needed, even if it does not extend beyond the patterns and assumptions of the local church they are part of.

TO THINK ABOUT

* In the church you go to, do you encourage people to try sharing the leadership of worship, or are your rotas set in stone and very closed to new people?
* Whose responsibility is it to identify such people, and give them suitable guidance and mentoring?[35]

Take me to your leader

One of the challenges in churches where the worship is dominated by a set of songs led by a worship band, is establishing who is the 'worship leader'. Is it the Reader or ordained minister who may be 'holding' the whole service (presiding, in the most general sense), doing the welcome and notices, maybe leading some prayers, introducing the preacher, leading us in the Lord's Prayer, helping us to respond to the sermon, possibly (if the service is eucharistic) presiding over the Lord's Supper itself, giving the final blessing and dismissal, and so on? Or is it the band leader, who sees him- or herself as the 'worship leader' (and maybe is seen in that way by others in the church), while the minister or Reader is seen as an 'add-on' who deals with the rest of the 'stuff' that has to happen?

---

35 For more on this, see Mark Earey, *Leading Worship*, GBW 152, 1999; and on the possibilities of sharing leadership, Trevor Lloyd and Anna de Lange, *How to Share the Leadership of Worship*, GBW 199, 2009.

Other models

The growth of Fresh Expressions of church means that often the existing models and patterns for leading worship need to be re-thought. If the pattern of worship itself feels different, then this may have implications for the leadership of that worship. More broadly, if the pattern of the life of the community being shaped into a church looks very different from inherited patterns of church, that will also have implications for how the connection is made between oversight of the life of the community and oversight of its worshipping life.

Another model which is sparking discussion is of 'curating' as a model of oversight of worship. This draws on models from the world of the arts, where someone 'curates' an art exhibition, focusing on creating the context, rather than determining the content. (See D4 Prophetic for more on curating and every-member ministry, and some of the implications for leaders.)[36]

TO THINK ABOUT

- Does the model of 'presiding' work for Messy Church? Does it work for café church?
- Does it work for other Fresh Expressions of church that you are aware of?
- Is 'curating worship' a particular form of presiding, or is it something completely different?

---

36 See also Mark Pierson, *The Art of Curating Worship*, Canterbury Press, 2012; and Jonny Baker (ed.), *Curating Worship*, SPCK, 2010.

TO THINK ABOUT

- What terminology is used for the leader/s of worship in your church?
- What training is given to those who regularly preach or take a leading role in worship?
- If you have a worship band or music group, how is their role (and the role of their leader) seen as part of the act of worship as a whole?
- How can we ensure that the way our worship is led (or 'facilitated') enables all to 'gather' and to know that they are part of a corporate act rather than a group of individuals offering their personal worship in the same space?
- How are those who lead worship in your church accountable to the church council or the annual meeting?

'Worship should be ...
or should involve ...'

B:

ROOTED IN THE WORD

B1

GOOD NEWS

Tom Wright starts his Lent book *Simply Good News* with three different exciting and dramatic scenarios of people bursting into a café shouting 'Good News' and then comments that we have lost both the sense of excitement about the gospel and also the fact that it is news.[37]

If you went into most churches today would you get the impression from the worship that people were excited by this news which was so good it was going to transform their futures and bring in a new world order? To some, 'Gospel' means simply the reading from one of the Gospels in the liturgy of the word, or even the large processional book from which they are read. To some others it refers only to a particular type of simple and clear preaching

> The word 'Gospel' probably comes from the Anglo-Saxon 'god' (meaning good) and 'spell' meaning to tell, the equivalent of the Greek *eu* (good) and *agello* (I announce) from which we get 'evangelism'.

which demands an individual response of faith. What a contrast to the church in Corinth, where Paul shows that it is not the particular reading or preaching, but the effect of what the whole church is doing in the whole of its worship, that opens the eyes of the unbeliever – so long as it can be understood.

---

37 N. T. Wright, *Simply Good News: Why the Gospel Is News and What Makes It Good*, HarperOne, 2015.

But if all prophesy, an unbeliever or outsider who enters is reproved by all and called to account by all. After the secrets of the unbeliever's heart are disclosed, that person will bow down before God and worship him, declaring, 'God is really among you.'
(1 Cor. 14.24, 25)

In what ways then should we expect our worship to be 'Gospel'? We talk about 'gospel truth' meaning something that is really, really true. That should be so in the case of our worship. God's complaints about the lack of integrity in the worship offered by his people are repeated by Christ in Matthew 15.7–9, and he says to the woman at the well, in their discussion about water supplies, 'God is spirit, and those who worship him must worship in the Spirit and in truth' (John 4.22–24).

We need to cultivate an attitude to worship which sees worship as proclamation – 'doing' the gospel. Our worship should embody – and make accessible – both the spirit and the truth of the gospel in a number of ways:

- in the evident integrity between the lives of the worshippers and the worship that is offered;
- in the relationships, shared peace and joy and devotion of those who are gathered;
- in the content and open style of the teaching and preaching;
- in the texts used in the service reflecting the Good News or the response to it;
- in the actions within the worship, from the openness of the welcome at and before the Gathering, through the Peace, to the open hands ready to receive the symbols of Christ's death and of our salvation;
- in the way the agenda for the church's meeting is set out, with a clear expectation of meeting God and being put right with both God and our fellow humans:

    when we assemble and meet together to render thanks for the great benefits that we have received at his hands, to set forth his most worthy praise, to hear his most holy Word, and to ask those things which are requisite and necessary, as well for the body as the soul. (Morning Prayer, Book of Common Prayer, 1662)

- in the use of interviews, drama and media clips to earth the challenge of the gospel;
- in the presentation, over time, of a wide range both of different ways of looking at what God offers, and of different responses to the challenge of the gospel.

All this requires not just energetic vision and consistent prayer but also patience and planning, contextual and expectant decision-making on the part of the whole church. And it requires vision and inspiration. St John's vision, relayed in Revelation chapters 4 and 5, which Tom Wright calls 'eavesdropping on a majestic mystery' and 'peeping into the very throne-room of God himself', conveys a sense of excitement at the immediacy of God's presence and at the total devotion of the worshippers, the crashing crowns of the elders conveying the noise of submission, of giving up of authority and power in order to be devoted to the worship of almighty God. And through this worship to end all worship echo those eternal refrains of the content and meaning of the gospel – the

'On this journey of faith we have no abiding city, for we have the promise of the heavenly Jerusalem, where the whole creation is brought to a new birth in the Holy Spirit. Here we are united in the company of all the faithful, and we look for the coming of the eternal kingdom.' CWCI, p. 161, Baptism and Confirmation, All Saints' Day until Advent

absolute glory of the God who created us, the sacrifice of the lamb, the creation of a new and holy people to worship God ...

You are worthy to take the scroll
and to open its seals,
for you were slaughtered and by your blood you ransomed
   for God

saints from every tribe and language and people and nation.
(Rev. 5.9)

That is where our worship should lead us. To heaven. With a
crowd of other people who have entered into the Good News,
into Jesus by faith, united with his death and resurrection.

What kind of God?

So worship leads us into God's presence. We hear and see and
are swept up in the experience of being with God, knowing God,
putting our faith in God, believing ... But what kind of God?
What is the picture of God we have in our minds? What is the
nature of this God whom we worship?

 Part of the Good News is that God is just so
varied. OK – God doesn't change, but the multi-
faceted nature of God enables people of all sorts,
backgrounds, needs, experiences, to meet Father,
Son, Spirit – whoever. And that can happen in the
worship in just one congregation as well as all over the world.

Think about it for a moment. Analyse it. Our worship should
enable us to meet God as Trinity.

- **Father,** encountering the loving father-heart of God.
- **Son,** rejoicing in being brothers and sisters of Christ, children
  and heirs of God himself (Rom. 8.14–17).
- **Spirit,** being, like St John, 'in the Spirit'.

And as each person of the Trinity has an effect on our lives, we
worship God as

- **Creator.** Sometimes we are overwhelmed by the sheer beauty
  of nature that God has created – mountains, mighty rivers,
  minute ants, the face or body of another human being: and
  we worship. (See box on creation at the end of B4 Believing.)
- **Redeemer.** Should our worship always be Christocentric? Is
  the incarnation (think of all those Christmas carols!) or the

cross more at the heart of our worship? Or is our focus on a risen saviour? Some hymns touch all these bases, and the seasonal patterns of the Church's year move us from one to the other.

- **Sustainer.** Meeting God the Holy Spirit is not just something we do in charismatic worship but continuously as the Spirit pervades our lives, gives us strength and enables our worship. (See B5 Filled with the Spirit.)

So our worship echoes and relates to the very nature of God. As well as being charismatic and Christocentric, our worship should – inevitably – be trinitarian, recognizing and valuing the part played by each person of the Trinity.

All this stuff about believing pervades all of our worship. As well as underlying all we sing and say and do, and the focus of our minds and hearts, it is also summed up and organized in the words of the liturgy, in the creeds and in the way many of the prefaces to the Eucharistic Prayer follow a creedal and sometimes trinitarian pattern. In what follows we look at the way our worship is rooted in scripture and in the Church's tradition, in the more formal expression of what we believe.

B2

BIBLICAL

Where does our worship come from? From hearts and minds full of gratitude to God, reflecting and absorbing his glory as we are changed from one degree of glory to another. But why are we like that? Where does it come from? Talking about being 'rooted in the word' might take us back to that initial experience of hearing and responding to Jesus Christ of which Paul speaks in Romans 10:

> 'Everyone who calls on the name of the Lord shall be saved.' But how are they to call on one in whom they have not believed? And how are they to believe in one of whom they have never heard? And how are they to hear without someone to proclaim him? So faith comes from what is heard, and what is heard comes through the word of Christ. (Rom. 10.13, 14, 17)

It is not just the initial experience of faith that comes from being rooted in the word, but the ongoing experience of the individual Christian and the growing Church. Paul again, writing to the church at Colossae: 'Let the word of Christ dwell in you richly; teach and admonish one another in all wisdom; and with gratitude in your hearts sing psalms, hymns, and spiritual songs to God' (Col. 3.16). This is a picture of the word taking root in people as they minister to one another and praise God from overflowing hearts. Did Paul have a copy-and-paste facility available in his Roman jail, from which he also wrote to the church at Ephesus? We find an almost identical menu for worship in Ephesians 5.18, 19: 'Do not get drunk with wine, ... but be filled with the Spirit, as you sing psalms and hymns and spiritual songs among yourselves, singing and making melody to the Lord in your hearts'.

So our Christian worship needs faith, word and Spirit. In this section we explore some of that inter-relationship between worship, belief and doctrine, being biblical and being charismatic, and how that works in terms of what we teach and how we grow.

Being biblical

Cranmer's prayer book made full and rich use of scripture. Those who regularly used its patterns of prayers and services would absorb into their being not only the biblical texts from which the liturgy was hewn but also the biblical theology that crafted it. The faith of generations of Anglicans was consequently built on sound learning, but more than this it was a protection against the challenges to faith in its day both from Roman Catholicism on the one side and Puritanism on the other. What about formation today? What can we say about the faith formed on the liturgical diet of the *Common Worship* era or its ability to produce confident disciples of Christ adequately equipped to confront the challenges to Christian belief in the twenty-first century?

Let us look at three areas:

- Where do you find the biblical material in our worship?
- What impacts on how it is used?
- How can we make our use of the Bible more effective?

1 Where do you find the biblical material in our worship?

Scripture is located in six places within our worship services:

1   in the readings, whether chosen from the lectionary or by the service leader;
2   in the liturgical texts themselves;
3   in the hymns, songs, canticles, anthems and motets sung;

4 in the sermon as it draws on biblical texts beyond the readings;

5 in the extemporary material: prayers, worship leader's links and comments;

6 in the visual stories in stained glass, carvings, mosaics, pictures and banners.

1 *In the readings*

The most important place we encounter scripture in worship is when it is read aloud for the people gathered to hear. Reading aloud in public is so alien to our culture that we need to ask, 'Why?'

Why a lectionary?

- It is a pattern we see in scripture itself. Look at the Old Testament reforms that followed the discovery and public reading of the law, St Paul's encouragement to Timothy to 'give attention to the public reading of scripture' or Jesus reading from Isaiah in the Synagogue at Nazareth.[38]
- It gives a balanced diet of Old and New Testament readings.
- It rescues the congregation from a diet heavy with the minister's favourite passages and preoccupations.
- Over the three-year cycle it covers the key passages necessary to preach on a rich variety of themes, from salvation history to Christian living today.
- It enables the shared counter-cultural experience of reading aloud in public that week by week gathers people to focus together on a story, some historical event or practical teaching, to ask 'What is God saying to us in this?'

---

38 Neh. 8, 1 Tim. 4.13, Luke 4.16.

Lectionary principles

Lectionaries began as readings appropriate for particular seasons (Easter, Christmas, Pentecost) became customary and other
readings clustered around them. This thematic use of the Bible is
found around the major festivals in the *Common Worship* lectionary today. But it can be – and was – taken to extremes. This is what
Cranmer and others reacted against at the Reformation, abolish-
ing non-biblical 'Stories and Legends, with multitude of Responds,
Verses, vain repetitions, Commemorations' which broke up the pattern ordained by the ancient Fathers who 'so ordered the matter,
that all the whole Bible (or the greatest part thereof) should be
read over once every year'.[39]

So which principle? Thematic or semi-continuous? Cranmer's
pattern of reading whole books survived until 1980, when the Alternative Service Book provided a different theme, with scriptures
selected to suit it, for each Sunday. With *Common Worship* there
was a return to the Cranmerian principle as the Church adopted
– and slightly adapted – the Roman Catholic three-year lectionary
revised by the Consultation on Common Texts to provide semi-
continuous reading for the epistle as well as the Gospel.[40]

The ministry of the word is a key part of *Common Worship*
services, with the Lectionary providing space for Gospel, Epistle, Psalm and Old Testament reading. There is also freedom to
depart from the Lectionary at certain times and to select readings to accompany preaching and teaching themes relevant to
the congregation.[41]

---

39 Cranmer's Preface to the 1549 Book of Common Prayer, printed in
the BCP with the title Concerning the Service of the Church.

40 For further reading, see Trevor Lloyd, Peter Moger, Jane Sinclair
and Michael Vasey, *Introducing the New Lectionary – Getting the Bible
into Worship*, GBW 141, 1997; Anna de Lange and Liz Simpson, *How to
Read the Bible in Church*, GBW 177, 2003.

41 For more information and ideas on how to use the 'open season' in
the Lectionary, see *New Patterns for Worship* [NPW], pp. 103–23.

TO THINK ABOUT

- Should there be more encouragement (and help provided) for churches to use the 'open season' of lectionary intelligently and creatively?
- If the pressure of time (and potential boredom!) are a threat, what are the reasons why the readings in the Liturgy of the Word should not consist simply of the – often shorter – passage of the Bible to be used as the text for the sermon?

TO DISCUSS

- Does the Lectionary sometimes break stories up too much? Why not explore the possibilities of reading longer sections of the Bible in certain circumstances (like the reading of the Passion narrative on Palm Sunday) to tell a whole story?
- What can be done to increase Bible awareness and knowledge? Are people aware of how much of the Bible is not covered by the Sunday Lectionary?

2 In the liturgical texts

There is a huge quantity and a rich variety of biblical material incorporated into the *Common Worship* texts themselves. A read through the main and accompanying volumes opens to us Old and New Testament texts, Gospel and Epistles, Psalms and Prophets, Old and New Testament canticles. Those who argued that liturgy should move away from outdated biblical imagery and conform to the insights of biblical criticism appear to have lost the argument in *Common Worship*.[42]

---

42 Have a look at the 'Index of Biblical References' at the end of the CW main volume

TO THINK ABOUT

- How would such challenges be faced in the future?
- Are we equipping people with enough biblical knowledge to counter such pressures?

Which texts do worshippers remember? Are they those we hear regularly or those we speak ourselves because there is a disparity between the quantity spoken by the minister and that by the congregation? In a typical Order One Communion service the minister gets not only a majority of the words to say, but a larger proportion of these are directly from scripture than those spoken by the congregation. In more informal worship settings there may be few or no spoken liturgical words.

3 In the hymns, songs, canticles, anthems and motets sung

Common Worship has a wonderful variety of psalms and canticles, in the main and accompanying volumes. There is space for hymns, songs, motets and anthems. The full riches of the differing musical traditions are available for the minister or planning group to use.[43]

4 In the sermon as it draws on biblical texts beyond the readings

With falling levels of biblical knowledge in the culture at large, there has never been a greater need for good biblical preaching. *Common Worship* always gives opportunity for the preaching of a sermon: it is the responsibility of the minister to make the most of this opportunity.[44]

---

43 See C8 Musical, and Anne Harrison, *Recovering the Lord's Song: Getting Sung Scripture Back into Worship*, GBW 198, 2009.

44 See Phillip Tovey, *Preaching a Sermon Series with Common Worship*, GBW 178, 2004.

5 Extemporary material in worship, whether prayers, links or comments

A great chef can throw a bunch of apparently random ingredients together, put the mix in the oven and produce a tasty and properly cooked meal; most of us need a recipe book. The difficulty of not having a recipe book is each meal may become a one-pot chilli lacking subtlety, creativity and beauty, or perhaps the same good meal is served time after time.

6 In the visual arts

The golden mosaics on the walls of churches like St Mark's Basilica in Venice or Monreale Cathedral in Sicily tell the Bible story in pictures. Stained glass often fulfils a similar teaching function: look at the thirteenth century 'Poor Man's Bible' window in Canterbury Cathedral. Paintings, mosaic, carving, sculpture, tapestry and banners can all contribute.[45]

TO DISCUSS

- Should the Church today be investing more in the contemporary use of biblical material in the arts?
- Do you think the extempore and contemporary worship material, such as new songs, in your church is sufficiently biblical in content and in theology?
- If not, can anyone do anything about it?

2 What impacts on how the biblical material is used?

A number of competing dynamics influence how *Common Worship* is used. There are challenges from both outside and inside the church. Those from the world 'outside' include:

---

45 See Christopher Irvine, *The Art of God*, SPCK, 2005 – especially his virtual tour of Ravenna.

• *Time pressure*

A survey of worship pages on church websites will soon reveal those that advertise the length of the service. Everyone is busy. Time is the most precious commodity and consequently the time for worship is squeezed. Worship services are stripped down to the core minimum: look how many of the *Common Worship* guide books explain the minimum that needs to be included in a worship service.

• *Lower personal biblical knowledge*

Where previous generations would supplement the church scriptural diet with biblical material from daily Bible reading, personal or family devotions, now many regular churchgoers read the Bible once or less per week. The result of this is reduced biblical knowledge and a disconnection with words and images in the liturgical texts.

• *Less regular church attendance*

Church attendance has become less regular and it is not uncommon for the attendance pattern for those who come to church to be 25 per cent worship weekly, 25 per cent fortnightly, 25 per cent monthly and 25 per cent occasionally. In this scenario biblical literacy becomes one of a competing set of demands on the content when gathering for Sunday worship.

The Sunday meeting has not only to feed the soul, educate the faithful, recruit the volunteer, share important information, build community, include the children, it needs to do it in ways that are both attractive, entertaining and spiritually fulfilling. The church does this against the backdrop of a secular world that provides activity and performance that our resources cannot match.

Challenges from inside the church include:

• *Biblical hymns have been ditched for emotional songs*

The nature of contemporary and charismatic worship is that songs flow seamlessly into each other as the congregation moves from praise and worship of God to adoration and intimacy with God. As a consequence biblically based, theologically refined texts are replaced by song lyrics that may or may not be either. *Common Worship* texts undergo consideration and refinement by the Church before having a formational impact on congregation life. This is not so for songs which may look biblical in terms of language and images drawn on but be unbiblical in how those images are shaped to create theological content.

• *On the screen, then it's gone*

Where the words of the Bible reading are displayed digitally, usually the text size is such that only a part of the passage can be displayed at one time. The viewer cannot look back to sentences or words once the display moves on. This changes how we engage with texts but it also changes how the text engages with us. Although it is disconcerting to some for the congregation to be looking at their mobiles as the Bible is read, the advantage of Bible apps and pew Bibles is that listeners have a larger amount of text available to them and freedom and opportunity to explore those parts of the Bible reading that the Spirit highlights to them.

• *Decontextualizing scripture passages*

Thirty years ago the minister might have preached through 1 Corinthians on a Sunday evening. Each week he expounded a number of verses, sometimes a few, sometimes almost half a chapter; the sermons were 40 minutes long and after several months the congregation had a good understanding of the letter. Today patterns of church attendance make that type of sermon series and systematic preaching ineffective. Now individual passages are read and preached on as a stand-alone resource to convey key teachings and learning.

• *Cut-and-paste Bible readings*

The Lectionary has an annoying habit on occasions of cutting out verses and of producing edited highlight readings from some passages. Encouraging the congregation to use the pew Bibles and reading from a Bible rather than the printed Lectionary volume not only helps them to see the whole of the passage, it also helps to put readings into their context.

3 How can we make our use of the Bible more effective?

Two young people encounter an angry bear, and one of the youths stops to put on his running-shoes. The other youth asks, 'Why are you doing that? You will never outrun the bear', to which the first youth replies, 'I don't need to, I just need to outrun you.' The temptation for many churches is not to try to outrun the bear (to face the challenge of discipleship and mission) but to provide a more comfortable, better resourced, more culturally appropriate, more entertaining, more enjoyable version of church than St Sleeping on the Wolds down the road. We are in a competitive marketplace, but is the competition just the church down the road or the conflicting multiple demands and pressures of modern consumerist society?

The marketplace we are in is about ideas and allegiances. We want to focus on growing congregations of faithful disciples. That involves allowing scripture that is God-breathed and useful for teaching, rebuking and training in righteousness to shape and form their lives. Sometimes, in order to get there, we need to re-focus. Some years ago there was an article in the Bible Society's excellent *The Bible in Transmission* magazine with the title 'Doing the Lucozade thing'.

Lucozade, invented in 1927 by Newcastle chemist William Owen and marketed as a source of energy for people who were unwell, with the slogan, 'Lucozade aids recovery', had only a limited appeal by the 1980s. The company rebranded itself, using a new slogan, 'Lucozade replaces lost energy' and the power of association with sports figures like Daley Thompson, to promote itself to the sports performance market and gain a completely new customer base. Sales tripled between 1984 and 1989. Instead of a drink for the sick and enfeebled, the new image made it the drink of the athletic and beautiful. In the article, Kathy Hesler comments that we do a similar thing by associating the Bible with lifestyle issues so that people see the Bible through the filter of fashion, home, garden or sport: all we have done is to connect the world of the Bible with the worlds that people inhabit today. The fascinating thing now is that the reinvention process has moved on. The latest Lucozade move shifts the focus away from sports, youth and hangovers onto 'daily strivers' – ordinary people doing a good job who could just do with a bit more energy to 'Find your Flow'. So what happens if we associate the Bible message with the – sometimes exhausting – daily grind?[46]

TO THINK ABOUT

- Think about the different worlds people inhabit: which parts of the Bible might be relevant to their world?
- Discuss the same question with reference to the different elements in the daily lives of those around you.
- How can some of this be integrated into our worship?

Train those who read, share and discuss good practice and ideas, such as …

Announcing readings

One temptation for some readers is to treat the announcement of the scripture reading as the equivalent of the sprinters' starting pistol at the Olympics. Get into the stride of reading as fast as possible with the aim of getting to the finishing line in the shortest possible time. In some churches a one-sentence introduction or even the paragraph heading from the Bible suggests what to

46 https://www.biblesociety.org.uk/explore-the-bible/bible-in-transmission/.

look out for and incidentally gives a moment for those trying to find it in the pew Bible to do so. But beware the detailed introduction, 'There are three things to look for in this reading ...', which goes on to upstage the preacher.

Signposting

There are plenty of places in the liturgy where we quote directly from scripture. Where appropriate we can signpost these simple phrases, 'The Bible reminds us', 'The Bible promises', 'God's word tells us' (without overdoing it on any one occasion!). How many mourners at funerals have any idea where the opening sentences come from?

Revisiting song lyric sources

In contemporary worship songwriting there are seasons for imagery. One year we are all doing battle, marching in, claiming land, next we are waiting for rains in dry and parched lands, another we are standing by rivers, another we are waiting for God. Sometimes these pick up the mood and spiritual situation of key churches, conferences or movements. Equipping our worship leaders to appropriately point out to the congregation the biblical images and scripture passages that lyrics draw on helps the congregation to recognize the image's source and also enables the congregation to explore those scriptures more fully for themselves.

Children

With so much *Common Worship* material to choose from, it is possible to have a unique liturgical service each week, but in services where many children are present, repeated liturgies are more easily learned. Making connections between liturgical texts and the Bible passages they draw on is good for the children and the adults. (See also A2 Caring and Inclusive and presentations using games, audio and videos in Scripture Union's *Guardians of Ancora* app. (http://guardiansofancora.com).

Reading the whole of a Gospel together

 Each year early in Holy Week we read that year's Gospel through in its entirety; usually there are 30 to 40 volunteers to read and others turn up to listen. Hearing a whole Gospel is incredibly powerful. It also trains the readers; to move speedily into place, not give unnecessary preambles before their reading, read at a steady pace, and to hear themselves in the light of listening to others.

B3

USING THE PSALMS

Losing the treasure?

'Whenever the Psalter is abandoned, an incomparable treasure is
lost to the Christian church. With its recovery will come unexpected power.' Dietrich Bonhoeffer's words are as pertinent
today as they were in the 1940s. Within evangelical churches,
which have seen prolific growth, it is rare to find psalms read in
services, unless part of a sermon series, and even less frequently
sung. Verses from the psalms might be read to introduce elements of the liturgy as a call to worship, invitation to confession
or assurance of forgiveness, or songs might be chosen which
occasionally include images and phrases drawn loosely from
the psalms. This unprecedented situation transcends denomin-
ational boundaries. Uprooted from the psalms, we are left with
a truncated view of God and his saving work in Jesus Christ,
impoverished corporate and individual praise and prayer, and a
generation ill-equipped to deal with suffering.

Receiving the treasure: the psalms in scripture and tradition

God's covenant people down the ages and throughout the world
have consistently found the psalms to be a source of great power.
The restoration of the psalms to the whole Church has been a
priority in times of reform and renewal, and the Church has
devised a diverse array of methods for their performance.

The psalms emerged out of the worship of God's people under
the old covenant, and it seems certain the psalms were used in

the worship of the Second Temple, especially at the annual feasts, and in the Synagogue. The Christian Church inherited this practice of singing psalms, which we glimpse in the gathering of the church in Acts 4.24–26 and Paul's exhortations to the Ephesians and Colossians.

> Be filled with the Spirit as you sing psalms and hymns and spiritual songs among yourselves, singing and making melody to the Lord in your hearts. (Eph. 5.19)

> Let the word of Christ dwell in you richly; teach and admonish one another in all wisdom; and with gratitude in your hearts sing psalms, hymns, and spiritual songs to God. (Col. 3.16)

Reciting and singing psalms became a regular feature of Eucharistic worship in the late fourth and early fifth centuries following monastic renewal. Within the daily office in both the West and East, the whole Psalter was sung, in some cases as frequently as every week. At the time of the Reformation, the Church of England in particular retained a semi-monastic daily office of morning and evening prayer emphasizing scripture and psalmody not only for the parish priest, but for all who desired to hear God's word and pray. On the continent and in England, metrical versions of the psalms made for congregational singing put the psalms back in the hearts and mouths of the people, shaping their corporate and individual prayer.

TO THINK ABOUT

- How often do psalms currently feature in your church's corporate worship or your own private devotion?
- Discuss what form this takes.

Esteeming the treasure: recapturing our hearts through the psalms

I have been accustomed to call this book, I think not inappropriately, 'An Anatomy of all the Parts of the Soul'; for there is not an emotion of which one can be conscious that is not here represented as in a mirror. Or rather, the Holy Spirit has here drawn to life all the griefs, sorrows, fears, doubts, hopes, cares, perplexities, in short, all the distracting emotions with which the minds of men are wont to be agitated ... It is by perusing these inspired compositions that men will be most effectually awakened to a sense of their maladies, and at the same time, instructed in seeking remedies for their cure.[47]

The Church has recognized the psalms as a mirror reflecting universal human experience which transcends time and space, and a medicine for the sickness of the soul. They both disclose and direct our emotions. They show us first the state of our own heart and awaken us to our plight, then present us with the character, acts and promises of God to recapture our hearts and move us to prayer and praise.

The psalms confront us with our mortality and transience in the light of God's eternity (e.g. Ps. 90, 102, 103). While celebrating God's good purposes for humanity (Ps. 8), they also portray humanity's intrinsic sinfulness, in which we share, alongside ancient Israel in her unfaithfulness to the covenant, (e.g. Ps. 51, 78, 106). Yet the psalms also present a God who does not abandon sinful people. They look back to God's redemption of Israel (e.g. Ps. 105, 136) and forward to the fulfilment of his promises to bless the world through Abraham's descendants through the provision of a king from within

'The psalms invite their singers to live at the crossroads of time, space, and matter.'[48]

47 John Calvin, *Commentary on the Book of Psalms*, Vol. 1.
48 N. T. Wright, *Finding God in the Psalms: Sing, Pray, Live*, SPCK, 2014.

the nation (e.g. Ps. 2, 18, 21, 72, 110). In the meantime, we are invited to receive forgiveness from the God who is gracious and wait for the joy of restoration and worship (e.g. Ps. 32, 51, 103, 130).

> Hide your face from my sins,
> and blot out all my iniquities.
> Create in me a clean heart, O God,
> and put a new and right spirit within me.
> Do not cast me away from your presence,
> and do not take your holy spirit from me.
> Restore to me the joy of your salvation ...
> O Lord, open my lips,
> and my mouth will declare your praise.
> (Ps. 51.9–12, 15)

The psalms show us a God who chooses to dwell among his people in one place on the earth – Jerusalem – and make it a place of refuge, justice and abundance from which his rule goes out (e.g. Ps. 48, 76, 84, many of the Songs of Ascents, Ps. 120–134), a foretaste of what he will do in the whole of creation. At the same time, they also express the anguish of living in a world where this is not always experienced (e.g. Ps. 42–43) and where this vision is violently opposed by enemies of God and of his people (e.g. Ps. 74, 79).

The psalms celebrate the goodness of God's material creation and his upholding of it (e.g. Ps. 65, 104, 145, 147, 148), including work and family life (e.g. Ps 127 and 128) yet they are honest about the chaotic forces that presently exist within it (e.g. Ps. 93) and look forward to God's coming to put everything right (e.g. Ps. 96, 98), a future which is bound up with God's promised king (Ps. 72). Human beings in a covenant relationship with God by faith are themselves being transformed by his word (e.g. Ps. 1, 19, 92, 112) and the psalms even hint at future resurrection (e.g. Psalm 16). The psalms keep us from denigrating matter on the one hand and deifying it on the other. Transcending these categories, the psalms ultimately present God himself, and not just his benefits, as the proper object of our desire and delight (e.g. Ps. 16, 63). He is our inheritance and our dwelling place (e.g. Ps. 91).

Jesus would have sung and prayed the psalms himself, and he and his earliest followers understood his identity and mission in terms of them. It is not just that certain psalms are obviously messianic, looking ahead to the coming of an ideal king or describing experiences which fit the pattern of events in Jesus' own life. More comprehensively, God's purposes for time, space and matter find their fulfilment in him.

> 'Much of the sweetness and beauty of the psalms lies in how they point us to the Messiah to come – Jesus Christ.'[49]

Jesus is the suffering king who brings blessing to the ends of the earth and judges the world in righteousness. He is the incarnate Son of God in whom earth meets heaven, fully embodying God's word in his perfect humanity, born of the matter of this world, which he took with him to the grave and brought out the other side in his resurrection.

> 'The story the psalms tell is the story Jesus came to complete.'[50]

TO THINK ABOUT

• Which truths about God, the world and human beings are emphasized in your church's music and liturgy? Which are not?

Lament

The image of living at the crossroads between the world as God intends it to be and the world as we experience it helps us to see how the psalms can contribute to the recovery of two important but neglected forms of prayer. The first is the lost art of lament.

---

49 Timothy Keller, *Prayer: Experiencing Awe and Intimacy with God,* Hodder and Stoughton, 2014.

50 N. T. Wright, *Finding God in the Psalms.*

There is seldom a place provided for lamentation in the Church, and down to the present day, many do not give sufferers the freedom to weep and cry out, 'Where are you, Lord? Why are you not helping me?'[51]

'When it came to expressions of pain and lament, we had very little vocabulary to give voice to our heart cries.'[52]

There is a strand of Christian spirituality which prizes the serene acceptance of God's will and creates the impression that the Christian life is one of unalloyed happiness. When events such as terrorist attacks or personal tragedies awaken us to the reality that the world is not as God intended it to be, contemporary Christian music can offer little help.

The psalms give us myriad examples of prayers of lament in a variety of circumstances – opposition, betrayal and persecution (e.g. Ps. 13, 55), deprivation of health and material goods (e.g. Ps. 6, 38), isolation (e.g. Ps. 39, 79). While most psalms end with a note of praise or expectation of deliverance, Psalms 39 and 88 end with no hope at all. Yet to bring one's complaint before God even in such circumstances is itself an act of faith.

'There is no better place to wait for God than deep inside the Psalter.'[53]

TO THINK ABOUT

- Which emotions are expressed in your church's songs?
- Who needs to be given the space and language to lament in worship?

---

51 Timothy Keller, *Walking with God through Pain and Suffering*, Hodder & Stoughton, 2013.

52 Matt and Beth Redman, songwriters, after 9/11, *Blessed Be Your Name: Worshipping God on the Road Marked with Suffering*, Gospel Light, 2008.

53 Timothy Keller, *Walking with God*.

- Is the general tone of CW (or your church's worship) too 'comfortable' to allow space for facing disaster, despair and lament?

Imprecation

The second neglected form of prayer which the psalms in their position at the crossroads help us to recover is imprecation, praying for God to act in judgement against individuals and groups. One helpful and widely adopted approach is to apply the reference to enemies who seek to harm the psalmist to the enemies of the world, the flesh and the devil which threaten to destroy us. It may also help to understand that these prayers arise in response to violent opposition to God, his justice and his purpose to bless the world through his people and his chosen king, rather than individual grievances; they reflect an eschatological stance in which our viewpoint is perfectly aligned with God's. In this, the imprecatory psalms are no different from the cry of the martyrs under the altar in heaven in Revelation 6.10 for God to judge the inhabitants of the earth and avenge their blood. While the imprecatory psalms do not sanctify resentment and vindictiveness as a reaction to private injury, the prayer that God would break the teeth of the wicked seems a legitimate response to, for instance, the horrors of child sex trafficking, and the increasing violence, torture and brutal martyrdom faced by our brothers and sisters globally.

TO THINK ABOUT

- When might imprecation be appropriate?
- What attitudes do we need to guard against if we are to pray the imprecatory psalms?

Poetry

A distinctive feature of the psalms which contributes enormously to their power compared to other types of biblical writing such as narrative or epistle is their genre as poetry. They share elements which are common to all forms of poetry: they are rich in simile and metaphor. The righteous person is a well-watered fruitful tree (Ps. 1) while the ungodly are strong bulls, roaring lions and dogs (Ps. 22). God is a hiding-place, a stronghold; he shelters his people under his wings (Ps. 91). Panting like a deer for streams of water (Ps. 42) conveys desire for God so much more profoundly than 'I'm desperate for you, Lord'. Perhaps the most characteristic feature of Hebrew poetry is parallelism, in which the second (and sometimes third) part of a line often develops meaning and structure in a more heightened or concrete direction. The result is an articulation of emotion, experience and divine and human character, experience and emotion, with a far greater vividness and density of meaning than prose.

Recovering the treasure: using the psalms today

There are several points at which the psalms can be woven back into corporate worship. (See also C8 Musical.)

- They can function as opening canticles, evoking the presence of God, like Psalm 95 at Morning Prayer in the BCP, reflecting much earlier practice.
- The psalm may be used as a reading in its own right.
- It may function as a gradual psalm, offering a response to the other readings.
- Lectionary provision or pastoral choice may determine which psalms are used on a given occasion.
- Preaching on the psalms is strongly to be encouraged.
- Psalms may also be used in intercession, perhaps read and then paraphrased or used as a springboard for supplication in light of the concerns of individuals, the congregation, the local community, the nation and the world.

- Psalms can also simply be used as alternatives to hymns and songs throughout the liturgy.

Recent scholarship encourages us to pay attention to the canonical arrangement of the psalms and not just see them as a random assortment. It is difficult, although not impossible, to achieve this on a weekly basis, and perhaps a return to the Daily Office needs to be encouraged, either corporately or individually. The CW Lectionary broadly facilitates this at certain times of the year at Morning and Evening Prayer, but this could be strengthened, especially in the Sunday provision, while recognizing the relevance of certain psalms to aspects of Christ's work celebrated at particular times of the liturgical year.

'We should say or sing the puzzling and disturbing bits along with the easy and 'nice' ones. We should allow the flow and balance of the entire set to make their points, with the sharp highs and lows of the Psalter all there to express and embody the highs and lows of all human life, of our own human lives.'[54]

The psalms can be used in worship in a diversity of ways. They can be read with increasing degrees of congregational involvement. They may simply be read by an individual, like any other reading. They can be read responsorially, with a lector and the rest of the congregation reading alternate verses and half-verses, or a lector can read the verses of the psalm while the congregation joins in with a refrain every few verses or so. The psalms can also be read antiphonally, with the two halves of the congregation reading alternate verses or half-verses. The latter opens up possibilities for the creative use of space. One half of the community could face the other, an arrangement originating in monastic communities, implementing in a very visible way Paul's injunction to teach and admonish one another with psalms (Col. 3.16).

---

54 Tom Wright, *Finding God in the Psalms*.

To exploit the full power of the psalms, we will want to follow the lead of the reformers in encouraging a return to congregational psalm singing. (See C8 Musical for more detail on this.)

Metrical versions of psalms are available which can be sung to familiar tunes. A number of songwriters such as Stuart Townend have produced versions of psalms in a contemporary musical idiom. For trained choirs, versions of psalm chant have been produced from the late sixteenth century onwards, while in the nineteenth century in England, under the influence of the Tractarian movement, efforts were made to introduce congregational chanted psalmody based on the Gregorian chant tones. More recently, responsorial forms of psalm chant have been devised, in which verses are sung by an individual or choir interspersed with a congregational refrain. The merit of chant is that it preserves the poetry of the psalms, which is often lost in metrical paraphrases, but adequate preparation and resources are necessary for a congregation to attempt chanting to good effect.

TO THINK ABOUT

- In what ways could psalms be incorporated into corporate worship in your church and into your own devotional life?
- Which musical arrangements of psalms would be best suited for your congregation? Is there the willingness and ability to try something more adventurous?

B4

BELIEVING

Christian worship is a theological activity. Through its prayers, praises, teaching and symbolic action, liturgy articulates the Christian vision of God. As the Dutch Reformed philosopher and theologian Gerardus van der Leeuw states, 'It is impossible to take the finger of liturgy without grasping the whole fist of theology'.[55]

The often quoted Latin tag *lex orandi, lex credendi* ('the law of praying, the law of believing') captures in shorthand the mutual interdependence of prayer and belief. Belief about the God we worship will inform the way we approach God in prayer, and the words and forms of prayer will also inform what we believe about God. Anglicans know this instinctively. The Church of England has long held the view that its prayer books are the repository for the Church's doctrine.

> Canon A5, 'Of the doctrine of the Church of England' states that such doctrine 'is to be found in the Thirty-nine Articles of Religion, *The Book of Common Prayer*, and the Ordinal.'

The Anglican vision of common prayer, whether forged in the polemical and turbulent years of the English Reformation or contemporaneously in the so-called 'post-Christian' era of the present, rests upon the conviction that worship is the primary means by which Christians are united in both belief and prayer.

The collects and Eucharistic Prayers are two examples of how prayer and theology work together. In the collect form of prayer

---

55 Geradus van der Leeuw, *Religion in Essence and Manifestation*, Harper & Row, 1963.

the opening address to God expresses belief about God which in turn both evokes and circumscribes the nature of the prayer being offered. Here, the CW collect for the Second Sunday of Epiphany, with minimal effort, converts theology into prayer:

Almighty God,
in Christ you make all things new:
transform the poverty of our nature by the riches of your grace,
and in the renewal of our lives
make known your heavenly glory ...

The fact that Eucharistic Prayers have been the site of some of the most intense theological debates in the Church about the nature of the sacraments, salvation and faith is reason enough to regard them as theologically significant texts. They represent an articulation of God's salvation, whether it be the dense polemical form in the BCP ('who made there, by his one oblation of himself once offered, a full, perfect, and sufficient sacrifice, oblation, and satisfaction, for the sins of the whole world') or the more leisurely and expansive prayers of our contemporary Eucharistic Prayers, which typically thank God for his acts throughout salvation history. (See C3 Eucharistic.)

Creeds

The Creed was not part of the eucharistic liturgy until quite late. Its use was only regularized by Rome in the eleventh century, though it was in use in Constantinople in the early sixth century.

The presence of the creeds in Anglican worship (from the Latin, *credo*, meaning 'I believe') is symbolic of the strong connection between praying and believing. The Church of England's liturgy is home to the Apostles' Creed (Morning and Evening Prayer), the Nicene Creed (Eucharist) and the Athanasian Creed (which in the BCP is to be recited on major festivals). The link forged between belief and prayer by including creeds in public worship is worth examining in more detail, especially for the light it sheds upon the nature of our worship.

Doxology

The location of creeds in the church's worship cements the dynamic relationship between the church's confession of faith and its praise of God, summarized by the term 'doxology'.

In the liturgical environment the creeds are doxological texts, part of the long tradition of worship that both recites and celebrates the merciful and loving saving acts of God (e.g. Ps. 105, 106, 107). When the Nicene Creed became an established feature of the eucharistic liturgy in the sixth century commentators on the Eucharist immediately recognized its doxological character. Dionysius the Areopagite describes the Creed as 'the universal song of praise' and 'the catholic hymn'. Maximus the Confessor described the Nicene Creed as 'the thanksgiving for the manner of our salvation'.

The doxological character of the creeds is an invitation to explore their lyrical quality as they are recited in worship. Musical settings provide a chief means by which the lyrical quality of the creeds can be enhanced. Musical settings of the Creed, as highlighted in the RSCM publication *Music for Common Worship*,[56] vary from the simple chant of Merbecke's sixteenth-century setting of the Nicene Creed to the metrical hymn 'We believe in God the Father' written by Tim Dudley-Smith for *Common Worship*. Churches with sufficient musical expertise could consider commissioning settings that suit the musical culture of the local church.

> The word 'doxology' comes from the Greek *doxa* (glory) *logia* (words) and means giving glory or praise to God, as in 'Glory be ...'

Lyrical forms are not limited to musical accompaniment. In liturgical celebrations that are deeply rooted in oral traditions, a

---

56 J. Wardle (ed.), *Music for Common Worship I: Music for Sunday Services*, RSCM, 2000 – part of an ongoing series.

responsive form of communal theological or creedal affirmation is commonplace; for example, the dynamic interplay between preacher and congregation in Pentecostal worship where the preacher's faith statements are communally appropriated by congregational shouts of 'Amen' or 'Alleluia'. *Common Worship* provides a version of the same dynamic in the responsive versions of the Nicene and Apostles' Creeds in *New Patterns for Worship*.

Narrative

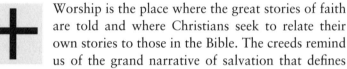 Worship is the place where the great stories of faith are told and where Christians seek to relate their own stories to those in the Bible. The creeds remind us of the grand narrative of salvation that defines Christian identity. As distinct from many church confessional documents, such as the 39 Articles of Religion, both the Apostles' Creed and Nicene Creed have a narrative thread that follows the unfolding of God's action in creation and redemption, revealing the trinitarian pattern of God's revelation as Father, Son and Spirit. The creeds derive their authority from being faithful renderings of the story of salvation, whose primary witness is scripture. In an age that celebrates the sharing of personal experience, the creeds tutor worshippers to enlarge their vision of the Christ whom they experience. Creedal recitation teaches us that our stories of Christ find their bearings and full meaning when related to the grand narrative of Christ's story.

The creeds find their liturgical counterpart in the Christian calendar. The ordering of the Church's year can be regarded as an exposition of the narrative shape of the creeds, beginning with the cycle of events around the incarnation, the passion and resurrection and then concluding with the season of the Spirit.

Confession of faith

The creeds are the voice of personal adherence to the gospel, a means to confess the faith into which we have been baptized. As Paul reminds those who have received the saving message of the gospel in first-century Rome, 'if you confess with your lips that Jesus is Lord and believe in your heart that God raised him from the dead, you will be saved' (Rom. 10.9). This verse neatly illustrates the vital link between verbal assent, personal faith and core content of the gospel that lies at the heart of any Christian celebration of God's salvation. The character of the Apostles' Creed, which originally developed from creedal statements that all candidates were asked to affirm at baptism, is an indelible witness to this action of confessing the faith as a sign of adherence to the gospel, 'the power of God for salvation to everyone who has faith' (Rom. 1.16). Creedal confession in worship is a recapitulation of the baptismal beginnings of Christian existence and an ongoing affirmation of the church as a community whose loyalty at all times and in places is to the living God. The oscillation between the use of the Apostles' Creed's 'I believe' and the Nicene Creed's 'We believe' represents the indispensable personal confession of faith that no one else can do for us with the corporate confession of faith that no individual Christian can do without.

TO DISCUSS

- Which aspects of Christian doctrine do you find most difficult to focus on when you are saying the Creed?
- Is it possible to focus equally on each phrase, or is it best to encourage people deliberately to vary what they focus on? What might determine this – how they are feeling or some teaching they have just heard?
- How do people avoid 'saying the Creed' being the recital of an empty form of words?

Creeds and tradition

The historical nature of creeds points us to the 'long-game' of Christian existence, witness and worship. The Church has always lived with challenges to its vision of God, no more so than in the modern era of gradual decline of confidence in our Christian inheritance. The Anglican apologist C. S. Lewis recognized that the most significant response to this contemporary challenge was the recovery of what he called 'Deep Church', a re-appropriation of the historical roots of Christianity.

Lewis understood the theological formulations of historic Christianity as foundational to the ecumenical agenda of the twentieth-century Church, the recovery of the body of Christ. The Nicene Creed, the result of the work of the fourth-century ecumenical councils, bears the marks of sustained debate about the relationship of the Son and Spirit to the Father. The formulations of belief were eventually agreed upon as a means of securing the unity of the Church. As an articulation of shared belief in what is distinctive and true about the Christian vision of God, the Nicene Creed has lodged itself as the primary creedal affirmation in the Eucharist, the sacrament of communion and unity in Christ. It is a reminder to us that the Church of England, which has always understood itself as part of the One, Holy, Catholic and Apostolic Church, belongs to a wider communion of churches who witness to the faith historically defined and situated in the ecumenical creeds.

It was the creeds and their orthodoxy that seized the attention and imagination of Lewis and his fellow apologists G. K. Chesterton and Dorothy Sayers as they commended a Christian vision of the world as simultaneously true and compelling. Liturgy is a bearer of orthodoxy (meaning literally giving 'right glory' to God) and is robustly conservative; it deals in tradition, the passing on of the faith that has been established from one generation to the next. Lewis's vision of Deep Church is encapsulated by the continued presence of creedal affirmation in worship. The creeds function as anchors, securing the Church to its historic orthodox moorings, as opposed to being 'tossed to and fro and blown about by every wind of doctrine' (Eph. 4.14). It is about 'not forgetting', and securing the faithful transmission of the faith, guarding the deposit of the gospel (2 Tim. 1.14).

Creeds and teaching

In his book *Praying the Eucharist* Charles Miller acknowledges that we often experience the Creed as 'a long concentrated theological statement in seemingly archaic prose'.[57] Its more un-familiar terminology is relegated to 'church-speak' in that it is safe to assume that the vicar understands but ordinary church folk don't need to worry about. It is highly unlikely, for instance, that the Nicene Creed's description of Jesus as 'begotten, not made' will fan the flames of heated debate over coffee after church.

However, the very fact that the Creed is a distilled summary of the Christian faith, and especially because it is couched in language that in some cases has lost its theological potency, points to the need for a supporting teaching ministry. 'A creed is a summary of faith. Each clause is a highly concentrated and highly charged "nucleus" of Christian thought and belief and experience' (Eric Abbott).

Hymnwriters, often the unrecognized educators in the Church, have long recognized the didactic value of the Apostles' Creed. Three of Mrs Alexander's most well-known hymns, 'All things bright and beautiful', 'Once in royal David's city' and 'There is a green hill far away', were written to teach children the meaning of the Apostles' Creed. The contemporary hymnwriters Stuart Townend and Keith Getty released an album, *The Apostles Creed*, with 12 hymns based on the creed (including the well-known 'In Christ Alone', and 'See What a Morning'). Hymnbook editors have organized hymns according to the structure of the Apostles' Creed, a most recent example being the RSCM/Canterbury Press publication *Sing Praise!*[58]

---

57 Charles Miller, *Praying the Eucharist*, SPCK, 1995.
58 Anne Harrison and Peter Moger (eds), *Sing Praise!*, Canterbury Press, 2010.

LThis link between the Church's worship and teaching is ancient, and rests upon the pastoral and educational demands of inducting converts into the faith, often originally called the 'mysteries', the deep meaning and logic of the salvation revealed in the performance of the liturgy. In a baptismal context, instruction on the Apostles' Creed has been a long established tradition in the Church. Work done by the Roman Catholic Church in its RCIA programme ('The Rite of Christian Initiation of Adults') has encouraged Anglicans to revisit their own baptismal teaching, and the recently published Pilgrim course,[59] a successor to the widely used Emmaus course, contains a concentrated section on the creeds, their history and meaning. This complements other excellent guides to creedal Christianity, such as Alistair McGrath's *Faith and Creeds* in his Christian Belief for Everyone series.[60]

The need to stimulate thinking and understanding of the creeds is no less important for those whose acquaintance with them has lasted for decades. The creeds are the fruit of extended theological debate in an era that took for granted that the true nature and content of the Christian of faith was always to be contested, whether in debates within the Church or in apologetics with non-Christian neighbours. Why should today's worshippers not similarly be encouraged to think deeply and ask questions about the God whom they name regularly in prayer as Father, Son and Holy Spirit? Over the past 50 years there has been resurgence in theological work on the doctrine of the Trinity, evoked by the intellectual and moral challenges and legacy of the twentieth century, which either implicitly or explicitly provide a means of exploring the trinitarian formulation in the creeds.

---

59 *Pilgrim: A Course for the Christian Journey*, Church House Publishing, 2016.

60 Alistair McGrath, *Faith and Creeds: A Guide for Study and Devotion*, Westminster John Knox Press, 2013.

Affirmations of Faith

The idea of using alternatives to the traditional creeds is not new. It may help those considering revisions in the future to consider the different possibilities:

- Extracts from the New Testament that articulate early church synopses of the faith (which in many cases were to form the basis for later creedal development). For example, those based on Ephesians 3, Philippians 2 or 1 Corinthians 15.3–7:

  > Christ died for our sins
  > in accordance with the Scriptures;
  > he was buried;
  > he was raised to life on the third day ...

- Paraphrases which amplify or explore the creeds, for example those in the *Private Prayers* of Lancelot Andrewes (1555–1626):

  > I believe, O Lord,
  > in Thee, Father, Word, Spirit, One God;
  > that by thy fatherly love and power
  > all things were created ...

  or Alan Gaunt in *New Prayers for Worship*:

  > We affirm our faith that God rules the world
  > in wisdom and goodness,
  > and that he has called us to be his servants ...[61]

- Paraphrases which shorten or simplify the creeds, such as the baptismal question-and-answer creeds in the CW Initiation Services.

---

61 Alan Gaunt, in *New Prayers for Worship*, John Paul the Preacher's Press, 1972.

- Metrical paraphrases such as that by Timothy Dudley-Smith noted above (the only one authorized), David Mowbray ('We believe in God Almighty, maker of the earth and sky'), or Michael Perry ('I believe in God the Father who created heaven and earth ...')[62]
- Affirmations suitable for particular seasons or occasions, such as this one in Trevor Lloyd, *Liturgy & Death*, GBW 28 (1974):

> We believe in one God,
> maker of heaven and earth,
> who judges all men ...
> And as we live by faith in Jesus Christ
> we have no fear of death,
> for we know that nothing can divide us from his love ...

When the Church of England Liturgical Commission was considering the worship needs of Urban Priority Areas and family services in the 1980s, the group, responsible in the end for compiling *Patterns for Worship*,[63] had as one of its members Michael Perry, then secretary of the Jubilate Group and editor of the CPAS/Jubilate Hymns publication *Church Family Worship*, so the wide range of material in that resource was considered, and some found its way into *Patterns*. The Commission was concerned about introducing too much new creedal material at one go, but there were other items that could have been included and would merit consideration in the future, such as the trinitarian one from Titus 2 and 3:

> We trust in God the Father,
> Who has revealed his love and kindness to us,
> And in his mercy saved us ...

---

62 Jubilate Group, *Hymns for Today's Church*, Hodder & Stoughton, 1982: 10 and 434.

63 *Patterns for Worship*, Church House Publishing, 1989 and 1995. NPW, p. 159, suggests which Affirmations are a good fit for different seasons.

TO DISCUSS

- Are Affirmations of Faith to be regarded as authoritative bearers of belief by virtue of their apostolic origin, or are they ancillary texts to the creeds?
- When are Affirmations of Faith best used?
- Why do Affirmations of Faith need to be authorized and should there be a limit on the number authorized?

We believe in God the Creator

God created us and our world: 'God saw everything that he had made, and indeed, it was very good' (Gen. 1.21). What impact does this have on how we worship?

- On earth, as in heaven, acknowledging God's creation leads to adoration.
  You are worthy, our Lord and God,
  to receive glory and honour and power
  for you created all things,
  and by your will they existed and were created (Rev. 4.11).
- We should be caring for the earth, working with God to sustain it – and humanity – for future generations (Ps. 104.14–16).
- We need to recognize the damage we have done to the earth:

  This sister now cries out to us because of the harm we have inflicted on her by our irresponsible use and abuse of the goods with which God has endowed her. We have come to see ourselves as her lords and masters, entitled to plunder her at will. The violence present in our hearts, wounded by sin, is also reflected in the symptoms of sickness evident in the soil, in the water, in the air and in all forms of life. This is why the earth herself, burdened and laid waste, is among the most abandoned and maltreated of our poor; she 'groans in travail' (Rom. 8.22).[64]

---

64 Pope Francis' Papal Encyclical, *Laudato Si*, May 2015.

- We live in a society that is quite rightly eco-conscious, and we should be providing models of good practice if we claim to worship a creator God.[65]

> God said, 'Let there be lights in the sky
> to separate the day and the night.'
> We thank you for the warmth of the sun,
> the light of the moon, the glory of the stars.
> We praise you for the formations of clouds,
> the radiance of dawn and sunset.
> Save us from wasting or abusing the energy
> on which all life depends.
> Open our eyes to behold your beauty,
> and our lips to praise your name.[66]

How might this affect how we worship?

This is a good illustration of the symbiotic relationship between what we believe (in this case, about God and the planet), and how we worship, which then affects how we live. It's not just a matter of a few prayers about ecological issues, but a sustainability audit of all our activity: our use of space, building design, heating, refreshments, water, as we catch and live out a model of sustainable living.

TO THINK ABOUT

- Make a list of things to consider if the church is going to live more sustainably. How might these affect our worship? For example:
  - how we use and share our buildings: what is the effect of working with other groups in the community?
  - where our food and drink come from: Fairtrade (is there space for a stall in church?) and local producers?
  - conserving energy and water, recycling responsibly.

---

65 For further reading: Dave Bookless, *Planetwise: Dare to Care for God's World*, InterVarsity Press, 2008.

66 *Common Worship Times & Seasons* [CWTS], p. 601.

- Think about how the different issues interact with each other and impact on the worship, image and mission of the church. For instance, should we save energy by reverting to hand pumping the bellows for the organ? How does that compare with encouraging toilet twinning or getting people to pay for the church floodlighting in memory of a loved one? And how do you include things like this in the intercessions?
- Should we make more use of the natural world, going beyond the flower-arrangers' rota to establishing an eco-friendly area of the churchyard and an annual celebration of it? Can we use the natural resources we have in our worship, to decorate the church or to use as focus for prayer and reflection? Some churches have used their land for community gardens, orchards or quiet green spaces. Are there ways of opening up churchyards to share the host of wildlife within them with others? And how can we build on things like that to enthuse a new generation to look with amazement at the natural world, sharing our wonder at what God has done and at how much we mess it up?

Celebrating the seasons

All this is too big and important to be encapsulated in Harvest Festival. Some have suggested that there should be a creation season for a month from the beginning of September, but it is in the nature of creation that it changes seasonally, and our worship should echo that. There are resources around that can help us share our faith in a creator God who is still involved in creation. CWTS has services for Plough Sunday, Lammas, Rogationtide and Harvest.[67]

---

67 See also Trevor Lloyd, *How to Plan Seasonal Events – A Drama in Five Acts*, GBW 202, 2006; and Season of Creation, an ecumenical website (http://seasonofcreation.org/liturgical-resources/) aimed at the month of September but with resources from a wide range of church and other organizations which can be used at any time.

B5

FILLED WITH THE SPIRIT

It is an open question as to whether the changes in the Church of England's worship over the past 50 years owe as much to the influence of the Charismatic Movement as they do to the liturgical revisions now authorized in *Common Worship*. Less speculatively, and surprising to some, it is possible to recognize similarities between the values that shape modern liturgical revision, fostered originally in the early twentieth-century Liturgical Movement, and the liturgical instincts of the Charismatic Movement. A recovery of the rightful place of the baptized to offer worship through the meaningful and active participation of the whole congregation, the hallmark of worship for the Liturgical Movement, has been encouraged in the Charismatic Movement by a creative appropriation of the biblical vision of the Church as the body of Christ, whose members are gifted by the Spirit for the benefit of the assembled congregation. Greater lay participation in worship, witnessed in the laity reading the Bible, leading intercessions, leading offertory processions and offering a ministry of welcome, are accompanied by charismatic practices of gifts such as speaking and singing in tongues, words of knowledge and prayer for healing. The recognition of the crucial role of music in enabling the full participation of all has been expressed by charismatics in the appropriation of popular music for worship. Songwriters, advances in recording techniques and means of distributing 'live' worship music and the development of the local church 'worship band' have all had an extraordinarily widespread effect on how congregations now sing in worship and the repertoire of songs and hymns available.

The large degree of overlap between these two processes of liturgical renewal can be read in the nature of revised liturgical texts. When the Alternative Service Book 1980 was published there was much that charismatic Anglicans could recognize as a liturgical expression of their experience of worship. In the Eucharist, for example, the introduction of the Peace with its liturgical claim that 'We are the body of Christ and by one Spirit we were all baptized into one body' combined with the gestures of peace-giving to sum up the heart of charismatic spirituality: the recognition and welcome of worshippers as fellow members of the body of Christ, animated by the Spirit to be embraced (literally!) through varied forms of informal gestures of greeting. The opening greeting of the president in the Eucharistic Prayer, 'The Lord is here; His Spirit is with us' (unique at that time among all the Eastern and Western liturgical traditions) articulates the fundamental belief of charismatics that assembling for worship is both recognition and celebration of the indwelling of God among the Church.

It is perhaps no accident that the origins of the charismatic movement should coincide with the social and cultural upheavals of the 1960s. As society witnessed a rise in popular culture, the loosening of established conventions and a new openness to Eastern mystical traditions, so there grew a grassroots Christian movement that was to promote immediacy in Christian experience of God in its doctrine of baptism in the Spirit, find new expressions of speech and bodily gesture in worship, and emphasize the importance of community in worship. However, the full significance of the movement for worship can best be appreciated with a much longer-term inheritance in view. The early 1960s also saw the first substantial moves towards revision of the Book of Common Prayer that was to lead to the ASB. As official revision began to conceive of experimental alternative services quite independently the Charismatic Movement was to offer patterns of public and personal prayer that contrasted most sharply with a Prayer Book whose language of prayer spoke of the Holy Spirit in whispered tones. The main emphasis of this chapter is to highlight ways in which the theological legacy of the Charismatic Movement is best understood as a retrieval of worship as 'in the Spirit', or perhaps more fundamentally to recover a way of naming 'God at work' in our worship.

Naming the Trinity in prayer
(See B1 Good News, 'What kind of God?')

> And because you are children, God has sent the Spirit of his Son into our hearts, crying, 'Abba! Father!' (Gal. 4. 6)

This pithy New Testament summary of Christian prayer brings into neat focus the way in which God is the inner dynamic of worship. The Spirit is sent to help us inhabit the pattern of the Son's life of worship, most clearly articulated in the naming of God as Father, 'Abba', and witnessed in his self-offering to God the Father through his passion and resurrection. Christian worship, thus shaped, is the approach to God the Father with, in and through the Son (as expressed in the concluding doxologies of contemporary eucharistic prayers). The Spirit is sent, furthermore, to enable Christians to offer worship; the Spirit empowers our cries to God, uniting them to the ongoing prayer of Christ as we, members of the body of Christ, seek to give glory to God the Father.

Thus worship is an all-encompassing participation in the trinitarian life of God, by the agency of the Spirit joining us to Christ, leading us in thanksgiving to the Father. This is what 'charismatic' worship is and why all worship is ultimately *charismatic* as well as Christ centred. (See B4 Believing.)

Let us trace this through four areas of charismatic worship.

Prayer and praise

In worship the Spirit works through enabling two key responses: prayer and praise.

Prayer is most obviously a central part of gathered worship – whether spoken or sung. As Galatians 4.6 shows, its character is determined by the life of God that the Spirit mediates to us. It is the language of the Christian family, naming God as Father. When we don't know what to pray, it is the Spirit who helps us in our weakness (Rom. 8.26) and it is the Spirit who reveals the deep things of the Father's heart to us (John 16.13–15). Worship in the Spirit is *relational*, drawing us into the communion of the God of love.

The Spirit also plays a key role in releasing a specific form of prayer: thanksgiving and praise. Look at what Paul says in Ephesians 5.18–20.

> Do not get drunk on wine, for that is debauchery, but be filled with the Spirit, as you sing psalms and hymns and spiritual songs among yourselves, singing and making melody to the Lord in your hearts, giving thanks to God the Father at all times and for everything, in the name of our Lord Jesus Christ.

The evocative contrast between drunkenness and being filled with the Spirit draws attention to the way the Spirit's fullness is marked by integration into a community of praise, the opposite of the disintegration that accompanies alcohol's excess. As we are filled with the Spirit, our tongues are loosened to give thanks to the Father for all he has done in and through Jesus Christ, and the gift of worship is learning how to share language in a way that intensifies and deepens the life of praise. The notable feature of the inaugural Spirit-filled community at Pentecost was its varied, rich and comprehensive articulation of the 'wonders of God' (Acts 2.4–12).

Gifts and participation

1 Corinthians 10—14 is a rich quarry for finding apostolic instruction on early church worship. Liturgists have regularly raided 1 Corinthians 10 and 11 for sources on the tradition of the Eucharist, most particularly the character of the meal that Paul 'received from the Lord' (1 Cor. 11.23). Charismatics have gone to the later

chapters (12—14) and repeatedly excavated a seam of detailed instruction on the nature of gifts of the Spirit and their place in the Church.

These gifts, or 'manifestations' of God's presence at work in the congregation (1 Cor. 12.7), have been the identifying banner of the Charismatic Movement, most notably in its encouragement of speaking in tongues, prophecy, words of knowledge and gifts of healing. While the more ecstatic gifts have attracted attention and controversy, the more significant feature of this appropriation of Paul's teaching on gifts is its emphasis upon the Church as the body of Christ and the Spirit as the common bond between each Christian. There are two aspects in particular that shape our understanding of the nature of worship. The first is that all who are baptized into Christ are bearers of the Spirit (1 Cor. 12.13) and thus gifted to participate in worship. The fundamental insight that becoming Christian is a conversion to a life as a 'liturgical being', a Spirit given capacity to freely offer gifts to God and others, lies at the heart of charismatic worship and more generally of Christian worship.

Second, worship is to be orchestrated in a manner that ensures that the offering of gifts, in whatever form, combines to 'build up the church' (1 Cor. 14. 3, 12, 26); the gifts of the Spirit are given 'for the common good' (1 Cor. 12.7).

Transformation

The Spirit is perfecting (to use a phrase of St Basil of Caesarea) the work of *resurrection* in the world. Worship 'in the Spirit' is part of the move of all of creation towards completion, asserting hope in the presence of all that remains to be redeemed. Thus, with Paul, worship articulates the groans of a creation subjected to frustration while also celebrating the 'first fruits' of the new order of restored humanity (Rom. 8.18–25).[68] (See box on creation at end of B4 Believing.)

---

68 Basil, *On the Holy Spirit*, 15.38.

Charismatic worship has encouraged a climate of faith and a culture of expectation that God is at work as we worship, bringing new life, healing and restoration. Yet patience in the continuing presence of disorder and death has been more difficult to practise, as critics of charismatic worship have highlighted; a movement that has reinvigorated confidence in the healing ministry would do well to recall that two of its founding fathers, David Watson and John Wimber, died of cancer in middle age.[69] (See C6 Seeking Wholeness.)

Perhaps the answer to this very Christian dilemma lies in the practice of intercession, not often identified or celebrated as a gift of the Spirit and yet very much at the heart of Paul's vision of Christian prayer. As Christians struggle with aspects of life that seem too bewildering and beyond God's help, the Spirit 'intercedes with sighs too deep for words' (Rom. 8.26).

Dependency

The German theologian Jürgen Moltmann highlighted the Spirit-centric aspect of worship when he said, 'The relation of the Church to the Holy Spirit is the relation of epiklesis, continual invocation of the Spirit'.[70]

In the Eucharist this is expressed in the invocation of the Spirit in the Eucharistic Prayer. As the reformer John Calvin once wrote: 'If the Spirit be lacking, the sacraments can accomplish nothing more in our minds than the splendour of the sun shining upon blind eyes, or a voice sounding in deaf ears'.[71]

The relationship of 'epiklesis' encapsulates the simple but transformational belief that Christian prayer is dependent upon the work of the Spirit. Charismatic worship similarly emphasizes the crucial dependency we have on the role of the Holy Spirit in

---

69 See Peter Cavenna, *The Healing Ministry of St Paul*, GB Renewal, 35, 200, pp. 18–25 on Paul as a wounded healer.

70 J. Moltman, *The Spirit of Life*, Fortress Press, 1991, p. 230.

71 John Calvin (1509–1564), *Institutes of the Christian Religion*, 4.14.9.

our worship. The Spirit is free and God is sovereign, therefore we need to remember:

> Human actions do not guarantee the working of the Spirit. The Spirit responds to human action, yet retains a freedom from human control. The Spirit works through us but is not controlled by us.[72]

Such a dependency requires that we nurture a posture of *openness* and *expectancy* in worship. Calling upon the Spirit is more than a liturgical technique or formula to be recited; it articulates the desire to be united in the communion of divine love that seeks our co-operation and transformation.

TO THINK ABOUT

- How are we to develop a repertoire of prayer and praise that enables a rich, varied and comprehensive celebration of God's being and action in the world?
- How are the gifts offered through our regular Christian worship to be recognized as 'spiritual'?
- How can the intercessions for this fallen world in our worship generate hope in the hearts of a congregation?
- How are we to foster a spirit of prayerful expectancy among the communities with whom we pray?

---

72 G. Tomlin, *The Prodigal Spirit*, Alpha International, 2011, p. 115.

B6

BUILDING AND FEEDING
THE BODY OF CHRIST

'So that the church may be built up.'
'Let all things be done for building up.'
'All things should be done decently and in order.'
'I received from the Lord what I also handed on to you.'
(1 Cor. 14.5, 26, 40; 1 Cor. 11.23)

These verses from 1 Corinthians reflect the tensions between worship being edifying and being orderly and accurately handed on. Edifying is about building up the body, the relationships within the church, the strengthening of the gifts of the body of Christ.

In 1 Corinthians Paul relates it to the use of spiritual gifts in worship, indicating that people overvaluing one gift can become exploitative of others, by not thinking about their growth and development. So in writing to this church which seems to have a very free charismatic style of worship, Paul has no hesitation about reminding them of the tradition that is received and which we need to pass on, as well as the need to have regard to one another and any unbelieving visitors. Cranmer quotes the same verses, but though he was bringing about a revolution in England's worship, setting the Church free from the unbiblical

> 'Edify' is to build a house (Latin, *aedes-facio*); morally, to build instruction in the mind methodically, like an architect. The scripture word 'edification' means the building up of believers in grace and holiness. (Eph. 2.21)

shackles of the past, he uses these verses to come down on the side of order:

> Let all things be done among you, saith S. Paul, in a seemly and due order. The appointment of which order pertaineth not to private men: therefore no man ought to take in hand, nor presume to ... alter any public or common order ... (1549 Preface, now 'Of Ceremonies'.)

Writing your own was not an option.

The two sides of this tension are not necessarily mutually exclusive, and in recent years there has been a finding of much freedom, within properly agreed frameworks. *Common Worship* has developed more freedom than any previous Church of England worship book. The Book of Common Prayer is very prescriptive in what should happen. It came from a much more hierarchical age. *Common Worship* in one way is more egalitarian. A variety of ministries is encouraged within the worship event and people are allowed to write parts of the liturgy themselves, for example the intercessions. In looking at the ethos of any one particular congregation the question of edification becomes quite central, because it is about the growth in faith of the members of the church, and about the mission of the church to outsiders.

So how do we expect the church's worship, its Sunday worship, meeting, event, agenda, to promote the growth both of the church and of its members?

> Disciples are sustained in their on-going Christian life not primarily through courses but through worship, mission and community – through being with Jesus and being sent out.[73]

As we reflect together on the Scriptures, God's word feeds us and we are changed. We become more like Christ in our daily living. As we receive Holy Communion we are spiritually nourished by Christ's body and blood. And we become what we eat.

---

73 GS 1977 *Developing Discipleship*, 2015, paragraph 19.

We are transformed into the Body of Christ and sent out to do his work in the world.[74]

TO THINK ABOUT

- Who are the 'disciples' in your church? What is involved in 'sustaining' them?

Building the Church

These questions of discipleship, formation, mission and growth have been on the Church's agenda for some time. We have a two-fold vision and mission. First (and this is the closest to Cranmer), to set the Church and its worship free, free to be honest about the world, our cultural contexts, our vulnerability, doubts and disagreements, free to be filled all over again by the Holy Spirit, in touch with our future as well as our past, so that every part of our worship brings people Good News, digestible and provocative Good News.[75]

Second, to take the good examples, vision and high standards exhibited in some places and to ensure that these are spread more widely and vigorously. This will involve not only things like training and envisioning local leaders, but care in making imaginative and bold appointments, a readiness to ditch things that aren't working in our context, and finding ways of focusing money and resources on the right things. Not everything in the list that follows – or any list – will work everywhere. But there is much going on that could be done better, or attempted in more places, building on others' experience. Here are eight things that work in building the Church:

---

74 Paul Bradshaw and Peter Moger (eds), *Worship Changes Lives*, Church House Publishing, 2008, p. 30.

75 See *Setting God's People Free*, GS 2056, 2017.

• Preaching[76]

Expository preaching, the systematic preaching through a book of the Bible, has its roots in the practice of the great preachers of the early centuries like Augustine and John Chrysostom, those of the Reformation like Martin Luther and John Calvin, those of the Puritan and evangelical revival like Richard Baxter, George Whitfield, Charles Wesley and Charles Simeon. While the thematic lectionary of ASB 1980 encouraged preachers to preach on a limited number of themes, the coming of the Revised Common Lectionary has encouraged the Church to do sermon series. These may follow one of the synoptic Gospels as the base Gospel for a whole year, use consecutive weeks on the Epistles, or explore the Old Testament, where the Lectionary allows either a reading which supports the New Testament lections or a series on its own. The coming of *Common Worship* gave further encouragement to this by indicating clearly that there is permission to depart from the Lectionary during Ordinary Time. Using this time for short series was given another boost in *New Patterns for Worship*, where the Liturgy of the Word section lists pages of ideas for sermon series with corresponding readings.

Some will raise objections to preaching series of sermons:

- 'It does not work nowadays when church attendance is erratic.' But if it works for some, and others start asking questions, that gives an opportunity for mutual ministry. If the sermons were that exciting, you can just imagine people asking the 'soap' question, 'What happened last week?'.
- 'It won't work in rural multi-parish benefices.' But this might give an opportunity for a team of preachers to prepare together on the same text, perhaps spending an evening on several sermons.
- 'What about some churches going at a different pace because they have only two services a month?' Does it matter? Or is

---

76 See also John Leach, *How to Preach Strategically*, GBW 211, 2012; Anna de Lange, *How to Engage with Scripture – With or Without a Preacher*, GBW 207, 2011; Phillip Tovey, *Preaching a Sermon Series with Common Worship*, GBW 178, 2004.

it an opportunity for an announcement, 'To hear the next instalment of this story, you'll have to go to St Dimwits-in-the-Marsh next Sunday, or download it from our Facebook page'?

Preaching need not mean one person standing up talking to a congregation. As Note 7 to A Service of the Word says, 'The term 'sermon' includes less formal exposition, the use of drama, interviews, discussion, audio-visuals and the insertion of hymns or other sections of the service between parts of the sermon'. The church of the future will be pushing these almost non-existent boundaries even further, with interactive sermons,[77] using Twitter lists and groups for real-time interaction with one another as part of the sermon, using similar means to distribute audio-visuals, breaking out into small groups with a number of simultaneous discussions or 'how-to' slots.

• Reading the Bible

Week by week hearing of scripture, (especially when the readings are sequential) enables people to begin to become familiar with the great passages and also to gain some sense of the over-arching narrative. (See B2 Biblical box on the Lectionary.) Hearing the Bible read is an important part of the learning going on in church and needs to be taken seriously. One of the strange ironies of the present time is that some churches which make a great deal of expository preaching have so little of the Bible actually read in their services. It is not just that there can be just one reading but that reading may be just one or a few verses. The church of the future, especially in an age of biblical illiteracy, will need to make space for having a good amount of scripture reading in services, and will be using innovative, multi-media ways of doing it, integrating it with the rest of the life of the church, in small groups or drama for instance.

---

77 Tim Stratford, *Interactive Preaching*, GBW 144, 1998.

• *Home groups*

Over the past 50 years mid-week home groups have become established in many churches. In some cases this is just for Lent (and sometimes Advent) but often they are a continuous part of the church's life. These groups can have multiple purposes: deepening fellowship, prayer and praise, but the focus is often on learning, using one of the many courses that are available, or material prepared locally.[78]

Some churches find it helpful to link home group study to the previous week's sermon, possibly with discussion questions prepared by the preacher. One of the major benefits is the simple fact of going over the material again. As one person said, 'If they get the same thing twice it has more chance of sticking'. Another major benefit is that in a small group more time can be spent on application.

One interesting example of this approach comes from a church where the minister preached through Psalm 73 over five weeks and the home group series was linked but used different passages of the Bible to deepen understanding. Here is a reply from one participant in one of the groups:

> We had our home group last night. I think the study went very well as everyone contributed to the discussion and applied it to their own lives. I asked what they thought of this style of study and we all agreed that we're really enjoying it.
>
> We like the focus on Psalm 73 and the way you're getting us to look at the other parts of the Bible to see the links with them. We think that because we're exploring the Psalm thoroughly the lessons we're learning are really sinking in so that we 'own' it and 'believe' it, seeing how it applies in our lives.

---

78 See for example, http://www.yorkcourses.co.uk or http://www.pilgrimcourse.org/the-course.

> We like the way you've set the study out in easy chunks. We also like the way the studies link with the sermons. Someone said that we can listen to an individual sermon sometimes which is very inspiring, but then can forget lots of it!! – Sorry! I know that's a sad fact. However, with this series of Bible studies linking to the sermons we feel we're learning more, especially because in the sermons you are reminding us of things you've gone into before.

Linking the home groups to the Sunday worship can also be done in various other ways:

- using responsive greetings which tie up with the theme or Bible passage, as suggested in the *New Patterns* section on the Liturgy of the Word mentioned above;[79]
- having a home group leading the intercessions, sharing something of their experience in prayer;
- producing a prayer board or a collage which people see as they enter, representing what the home groups have been doing.

• *All-age learning*

There is still a lively debate about all-age worship. While some people are heavily committed to all ages worshipping and learning together, others are much more sceptical. For example, Mark Woods in an article called 'Better Apart? Why all-age services might not be helping anyone'[80] highlights the uncomfortable truth that often they are a 'halfhearted compromise that pleases no-one'. Sadly there are not many clergy and Readers who have the skill to enable worship and teaching that speaks across the age range. And it is the experience of a significant number of congregations that where there are strong Sunday schools (or

---

79 NPW, p. 105.

80 http://www.christiantoday.com/article/better.apart.why.all.age.ser vices.might.not.be.helping.anyone/39333.htm: Mark Woods, Christian Today website (accessed 6 August 2014).

the equivalent) some families stay away when it is Family Service. That is in addition to the older adults who stay away from all-age worship because they see it as worship for the children. It is certainly worthwhile for a church to think carefully about whether all-age worship and teaching is the best way forward.

Messy Church can be seen as a slightly different approach to all-age worship. It does seek to allow all ages to take part in their different ways, but even here genuine worship (and learning) that meets the needs of all ages is very hard to attain.

Nevertheless most Churches do believe there is a value in all-age worship and learning, and Praxis training days that were run to help with this in recent years drew the largest attendance for Praxis training events for some time. This shows both the perceived value of all-age worship and learning, but also the desire to get help with it.[81]

TO DISCUSS

- Do you find people in your church grow in their faith more through preaching, Bible reading or home groups?
- Has there been any discussion or experience of all-age learning among members of the church?

Some churches have sought to ensure that what is taught from the pulpit also relates to what is learnt by the children in their own activities. For those who follow the Lectionary, the Roots worship and learning resources enable this to happen, and as well as the integrated *Light* material, Scripture Union produce books of all-age resources related to the CW Lectionary.[82]

---

81 For more resources, see www.messychurch.org.uk/ and http://www.praxisworship.org.uk/.

82 See https://www.rootsontheweb.com and www.scriptureunion.org.uk/Light.

• *Sunday school*

Sunday school for adults is different from 'all-age' learning and worship. It is interesting to note that all-age worship is not part of what is offered by many of the mega-churches in America (e.g. Willow Creek Community Church) where adults and children have their separate times every Sunday.

Where the children's activities run alongside the sermons, many bring the children in at the end of the service to share what they have been doing.

> We also link the Sunday school teaching to the sermon. And when the children come back into the service, we do the 'get them out to the front' thing. There is a lot of waving around of craft and colouring in, but it also gives me the opportunity to nail the main point in a very simple way for the adults when I quiz the children about what they have learnt.

Where there is no regular tie-in with the sermons taught, there can still be ways of bringing things together. For example, a monthly all-age service can build on what the children have been doing the previous weeks in their own groups.

• *Worship and learning in the home*

In Victorian times a key part of devotional life was worship in the home by the whole household together. This has virtually disappeared in the UK, largely because of cultural and time pressures. The one remnant which is still valuable and reasonably widespread is that of saying 'Grace' before meals. However, some still see worship as a family as an important dimension of worship and discipleship. This was very clearly an important part of life in biblical times. Some evangelical churches are trying to promote useful materials from America where this is more encouraged.[83]

---

83 For example, Jason Helopoulos, *Neglected Grace*, Christian Focus Publications, 2013.

Neglected Grace seeks to take seriously the pressures on family life, and insists that family worship be seen as an opportunity and a grace, not a means of increasing a sense of guilt. It is very practical, although not all will like the patriarchal approach taken by the book. The pattern encouraged is that of having a Bible reading, a prayer and a song or hymn, although the opportunity to expand this can be helpful on occasion.

In this country, encouragement of family worship has come from Stephen Cottrell in *How to Pray*.[84] He is very positive about the practice of praying at meal times, but notes:

> When I first started to explore ways of praying together at home with small children I looked around for books on the subject. I could not find any. There are plenty of books of prayer *for* children, but nothing about how to pray *with* children. Since then I have discovered one or two, but it still seems to be that this is a terribly neglected area of Christian formation. I think back to my own parish ministry and realise that I never gave any teaching, and very little encouragement, to families to pray together.

He goes on to make suggestions for a way forward for families, placing an emphasis on simple ritual as an important part of family worship. Perhaps with advocates from both the evangelical and catholic traditions we might yet see a fresh flourishing of family worship and prayer time, and it might be good if the Church of England could produce some simple resources to help with this.

- *Music* (See C8 Musical)

Music helps congregations to grow as they are bound together; it also helps individuals, who recall a particular truth or verse of scripture which has been embedded in them by music, often brought to mind in moments of tension, danger, depression and loneliness.

---

84 Stephen Cottrell, *How to Pray*, Church House Publishing, 2010.

• *Personal devotion*

Finally, there is the personal devotion, worship and learning of the individual Christian. This has survived better than family worship but is still a struggle for many Christians. Some have gone down the liturgical route of using daily prayer which has the value of substantial biblical input. The use of Bible reading notes produced by Scripture Union, the Bible Reading Fellowship and others is still very widespread. Where a church has a good number of members of a congregation using the same set of notes, then this can enrich and encourage considerably the personal time. All of these can now be accessed electronically through smart phones and tablets which is undoubtedly a great help for many. There are also digital and online resources, including podcasts, which are not available in paper media form. What is clear is that the variety is ever expanding and while this enables people to find what suits them, it raises the question of whether it is still possible to link individual devotion with the corporate.

TO DISCUSS

- When we evaluate worship should the formational impact of worship be among the criteria we should use?
- After a service, ask, did the worship build up the body?
- Did people leave feeling encouraged, or learning new things about the faith, or empowered to take action?
- Does this line of questioning need to be supplemented with questions about how this worship relates to the worship traditions (the 'handing on') of the church?
- Review this chapter and share one or two practical suggestions that might lead to development in your own church.

*'Worship should be ...
or should involve ...'*

C:
RESPONDING

C1

SACRAMENTAL

How do sign, symbol and sacrament contribute to our worship? Is sacramental worship comprised of sacraments, or worship which in its entirety is a sacrament? To answer such questions, we need to take a step back, and see where the concept of sacrament comes from and how it has developed.

Background

Human beings have used signs to communicate with one another since before history was recorded – the recording of history, of course, needs some system of signs.

In the Bible we find that God used both words and signs to communicate with human beings. The rainbow was a sign of God's covenant with Noah, and the manger was a sign for the shepherds to pinpoint the newborn Messiah (see Genesis 9.12 and Luke 2.12).

In the first three Gospels, we read of the Pharisees demanding a sign, and Jesus denying them any sign but 'the sign of Jonah', meaning his resurrection. However, John's Gospel is clear that the disciples are given a number of signs, the first being the provision of wine at a wedding celebration.

> Jesus did this, the first of his signs, in Cana of Galilee, and revealed his glory; and his disciples believed in him. (John 2.11)

Many anthropologists would make a distinction between a sign and a symbol, saying that a sign has one meaning conveying one piece of information, as seen for example with road signs where an arrow indicates direction, or a bar indicates 'No entry'. A symbol, on the other hand, has a variety of meanings all at once, so the Bethlehem manger is not only 'X marks the spot' for the shepherds, but can also speak to us of Christ's humility, and of him giving himself as sustenance. Although some have found this distinction helpful, we will not pursue it in this chapter, given that neither scripture nor ancient formularies of the Church respect it. Furthermore, any reflective thinker, or inventive preacher, can attribute extra meaning even to a road sign.[85]

Jesus was involved in a range of symbolic actions. Some of these were part of his Jewish background, such as his circumcision, presentation in the Temple, the Passover and other festivals. As we read the stories of his ministry we can perceive symbolism in many of the events: laying hands on the sick, being anointed with oil, washing the disciples' feet. At the end of his ministry, he specifically commanded his followers to baptize new disciples, and to consume bread and wine in his memory.

> People have different ways of learning: some take in new ideas more readily through images, while others prefer words.

The early Church

As the Christian Church took shape from the day of Pentecost onwards, the disciples were sustained in their lives by their faithfulness to the apostles' teaching, the first of the key features of church life listed in Acts 2.42. However, close upon the heels of teaching came community, and a community which shared the teaching is exactly the pattern we find in the early chapters of Acts, and again in 1 Corinthians 14, or, say, in brief compass in Colossians 3.15–17. This was not the interaction of faceless people texting

---

85 For more on this distinction between sign and symbol, see for example Victor Turner, *Forest of Symbols*, Cornell University Press, 1970; and Phillip Tovey, *Inculturation of Christian Worship: Exploring the Eucharist*, Ashgate, 2004.

or Tweeting; it was folk in actual company with each other, loving each other and building each other up with the word. And that, as Colossians 3.17 and other instances show, could include singing psalms and hymns, as well as telling the stories of Jesus and interpreting their situation to each other. They could see and touch one another: as when Peter signalled with a hand-gesture for silence (Acts 12.17), or the company shared a kiss when saying good-bye (Acts 20.37).

They laughed and frowned; they gestured and knelt; they communicated by the use of all five senses just as other communities do. They used the material world for special purposes, as in the baptism of new converts in water, and thereafter the 'breaking of bread' (Acts 2.42), both practised at Jesus' command (Matt. 28.19, 1 Cor. 11.24–25).

Teaching and community are sometimes referred to by the Greek words *didache* and *koinonia*.

The infant Church lived bodily in and with the physical world, seeing it as the instrument and vehicle of the power of the living God.

There is little doubt that the signs and ceremonies in use in the Church settled down in the early centuries into quite formal patterns. Church life is conservative, and, just as families find themselves with cycles of familiar routines (Sunday lunch, birthday cakes, hanging up stockings on Christmas Eve, etc.), so the 'liturgical' patterns of the early Church tended to run on for generations in each place. Some ceremonies grew in how they were valued (anointing is a good instance), others appeared for a while and then disappeared (giving milk and honey at baptismal eucharists in the third century, for example).

Ephrem the Syrian (c. 306–373) used symbols in nature and scripture as a part of his theology, which he constructs mostly in song. He sees a whole web of symbols created by God and as pointers back to God for the salvation of all people. There is a sense of wonder that the world around us and the scriptures as revealed to us constantly have an opening and unfolding as objects revealing the nature of God and his saving power in Jesus. These symbols give a deeper significance to the creation and the work of God and redemption. He often used the Syriac word *raza* for symbol. The solemn Holy Communion in the Syrian tradition is *raza*.[86]

Even though your symbol may be small,
yet it is a fountain of further mysteries.
Hymns on Faith 4.10

The term 'sacrament' came into use as a broad name for ceremonies. 'Sacrament' is not a biblical term (though the Vulgate used *sacramentum* where English Bibles have 'mystery' or 'secret' to translate *musterion* in Ephesians 5.32). In classical Latin it meant 'an oath', but in the Church the word took on a new meaning. Augustine of Hippo noted 30 'sacramenta' in use in his time, some of them fairly trivial by modern evaluation, for instance including not only baptism and eucharist, but also making the sign of the cross.

Augustine (354 to 430) was a professional orator who became Bishop of Hippo in northern Africa, and notable theologian of the first millennium.

This somewhat loose early church pattern was tightened and defined by Peter Lombard in his *Four Books of Sentences*, where he established some basic structuring criteria for sacraments – notably that a sacrament had an outward *sign*, a spoken *form* (i.e. formula), and a stated *benefit* (or 'inward grace'). Against these criteria he listed seven sacraments as the official such means of grace within the Church; and the Fourth Lateran Council in 1215, and later the Councils of Florence and Trent, confirmed this listing and it is integral to the body of Roman

Peter Lombard (c. 1096–1160) was a Christian scholar who became Bishop of Paris in the last year of his life.

---

86 Sebastian Brock, *The Luminous Eye: The Spiritual World Vision of Saint Ephrem,* Cistercian Publications, 1992, p. 56.

Catholic doctrine to this day. The seven were: baptism, confirmation, ordination, eucharist, penance, matrimony, and extreme unction. The first three of these were given once-for-all-for-life, and were represented as making a supposed indelible mark upon the soul.

The Reformation

The sixteenth-century reformers accepted only the two sacraments commanded by Jesus, baptism and Holy Communion. They stressed the promises of God associated with the symbol as the most important aspect of a sacrament. They did not negate the importance of the symbol. Indeed they saw a significant role for symbols in that our faith is weak and so God graciously gives us symbols to strengthen our faith to follow him. It is our weakness that makes us vulnerable to not simply believing the oral word, and it is God's graciousness that provides symbols to strengthen our weak faith.[87]

Out of this tradition comes the phrase 'effectual signs' which are used in the 39 Articles in discussing sacramental theology.

Article XXV

Of the Sacraments

Sacraments ordained of Christ be not only badges or tokens of Christian men's profession, but rather they be certain sure witnesses and effectual signs of grace and God's good will towards us, by the which He doth work invisibly in us, and doth not only quicken, but also strengthen and confirm, our faith in Him.

There are two Sacraments ordained of Christ our Lord in the Gospel, that is to say, Baptism and the Supper of the Lord.

---

87 For more detailed discussion of worship and the Reformation in England, see, for example, Colin Buchanan, *What Did Cranmer Think He Was Doing*, Grove Books, 1976; or Diarmaid MacCulloch, *Thomas Cranmer: A Life*, Yale, revised edition 2016.

> Those five, commonly called Sacraments, that is to say, Confirmation, Penance, Orders, Matrimony, and Extreme Unction, are not to be counted for Sacraments of the Gospel, being such as have grown partly of the corrupt following of the Apostles, partly are states of life allowed in the Scriptures; but yet have not the like nature of Sacraments with Baptism and the Lord's Supper, for that they have not any visible sign or ceremony ordained of God ...

The Article is clear that a sacrament is not only a sign or symbol, but it is a means by which God works within the recipient – a means of grace. Although the Article does not attribute this work to the Holy Spirit, this is implicit and is made explicit in the baptism service, and in the CW Order One Holy Communion services.

The *Thirty Nine Articles of Religion* were approved by the Parliament and Queen of England in 1571. They were intended to show the distinctive theological position of the Church of England and have normally been bound with printings of the 1662 BCP.

The wording of the Article narrows the use of the word 'sacrament', from its former wider usage, to the two sacraments commanded by Jesus. Later Church of England documents do not use the word 'sacrament' to refer to anything else. The Catechism in the 1662 Prayer Book, used to prepare people for confirmation, uses 'sacrament' to refer to baptism and Holy Communion only. The same is true of the Canons of the Church of England to this day.

Alongside the tighter definition of 'sacrament' the reformers reduced the number of other ceremonies which were customarily part of church life. An explanation of this, titled, 'Of ceremonies – why some be abolished, and some retained' was included in the 1549 and subsequent prayer books. The entire text is worth reading, but we quote here only one sentence:

> Christ's Gospel is not a Ceremonial Law, (as much of Moses' Law was,) but it is a Religion to serve God, not in bondage

of the figure or shadow, but in the
freedom of the Spirit; being content only with those Ceremonies
which do Serve to a decent Order
and godly Discipline, and such as
be apt to stir up the dull mind of

The next two chapters in
this book reflect further
on the two 'dominical'
sacraments.

man to the remembrance of his duty to God, by some notable
and special signification, whereby he might be edified.

More recent developments in England

While the formularies of the Church of England still have the
same balance and central teaching as in 1662, the nineteenth-
century Anglo-Catholic movement entrenched a principle, which
even others now tend to welcome, that what is not explicitly for-
bidden is implicitly allowed or even encouraged. We have then
five different categories of ceremonies.

- Two sacraments ordained by Christ.
- Ceremonial objects and actions required by the BCP, such as
  wedding rings and kneeling for prayer.
- Ceremonies from the ancient Church restored to optional use
  by *Common Worship* (or its provisional precursors), such as
  the sharing of the Peace, the use of ashes at the beginning of
  Lent, candles for Easter and Advent, and the use of oils in
  baptism.
- Other ancient objects and rituals in use but not officially
  sanctioned in our texts: altar frontals and candles, bells, processions, incense, statues, bowing to some objects and lifting
  others, making the sign of the cross, facing east when saying
  the Creed, a new incumbent ringing the church bell, etc.
- Newer ceremonies imported or created for a variety of reasons
  – medals for choir members, giving children grapes at the
  communion rail, lifting arms in the air ...

Some of these have deep meaning, and are adopted for that
reason, but need appropriate explanation to be understood.

Others, however, are used without reflection. Cranmer, looking critically at the Church of England today, would ask whether each is a burden that hampers lively faith, or a benefit which liberates and edifies.[88]

TO THINK ABOUT

- Reflect on your own church building and regular worship – and take nothing for granted, as though you were a visitor unacquainted with church. What questions would you ask? As the visitor's host would you be able to explain the origin and meaning of all objects and rituals?
- Which signs and symbols have particular significance for you as an individual? For the congregation with which you worship?

In the wider Anglican Communion

Engagement with symbols can be quite personal; the pebble picked up on the beach where you proposed to your spouse may sit in your home as a significant reminder of a special day. The use of symbols may also vary from congregation to congregation, and from country to country. In Christian worship corporate symbols can be adopted with meanings which reflect the local culture of the worshippers. There has been some considerable discussion about adapting worship to local cultures.[89]

- This can be seen for example in the Church of South India where in the marriage service a *mangalasutra* (a necklace with three knots) may be substituted for the more Western wedding ring.[90]

---

88 See John Leach, *How to Use Symbol and Action in Worship*, GBW 184, 2005.

89 See David Holeton (ed.), *Liturgical Inculturation in the Anglican Communion*, JLS 15, 1990.

90 Church of South India Prayer Book, 2004.

- In some places local customs have been included in the baptismal liturgy. For example, in Sri Lanka local birth customs can now be used to express new birth at baptism: oiling the body, striking the candidate with a broom (*ekel*), and making the sign of the cross in sandalwood paste.[91]
- In Uganda the book of Provisional Rites includes a Christian service of circumcision, a practice of some of the tribes of that country.

The incorporation of local customs into the liturgy has long been a practice of the Church. It has been argued that processions and incense are as much from the Roman imperial court as any other source and were reinterpreted in a Christian way as they became used in Christian worship. It is to be expected that such processes will continue today in the Church throughout the world.

Issues and questions for today and tomorrow

As we look to the future, there are some key issues for the whole Church to discuss.

For better or for worse

A periodic review of the use of symbols and the actions we do in worship is important. If much of our worship is static and the only major ceremonial is the collection, then it might appear that this is one of the most important events in the service. On the other hand, if our service is too full of meaning-rich ceremonial, will people get conceptual indigestion? A telescope used in the right way brings distant things closer; but used in the wrong way, makes them seem further away.

---

91 Church of Ceylon Baptism Service, 2013.

TO THINK ABOUT

At a local level (and perhaps also at national level), can you identify, for example:

- a core of vital (even if not commanded) ceremonies,
- a resource of other godly ones,
- a danger-list of misleading ones?

However, if we consider carefully the use of symbols throughout the whole service and their use in a powerful way, then maybe we will open ourselves to the ongoing revelation of God and draw nearer to God with our faith strengthened.

Change is here to stay

Symbols can seem to have a life of their own. They exist as a part of the corporate living nature of the Church. There are times when some symbols may be barely used at all, for example the use of liturgical dance which from time to time is resurrected and used in worship but at other times is forgotten. Symbols can also be reborn, as for example in the development of the Peace in modern worship, where the action of shaking hands has become very common, but still today many remember when there was no exchanging of the Peace. They can also die out, as, for example, the receiving of communion wine through a straw. Change is a part of the nature of symbols, and they can be living, fossil-ized, or dead. Then they become part of history of what we once did but no longer do. As we look to the future, we inevitably embark on a quest for new and edifying ceremonies. (See also A3 Creative. Pebbles, tea-lights, post-it notes and pipe-cleaners may be helpful the first time you use them – but can easily be over-done!)[92]

---

92 See Peter Craig-Wild, *Tools for Transformation*, DLT, 2002.

Do use words – they are necessary!

Symbols speak to us in a way that we cannot convey through words alone. They reach parts of our consciousness that are unreachable through verbal communication alone. Nevertheless, if they are to carry the right meaning, they must be explicitly linked to the word which they are meant to support. In the traditional Passover meal the ingredients were explained among the Jews. So, for instance, we mark a baptismal candidate with the sign of the cross, saying, 'Christ claims you for his own. Receive the sign of his cross' and follow it with, 'Do not be ashamed to confess the faith of Christ crucified'.

There is an intriguing question as to whether there are any wordless signs or ceremonies which are so self-explanatory that they do not need verbal interpretation. There is one possible example in the sphere of 'upness' and 'downness' – to kneel or fall down before someone is to acknowledge that person's 'superiority' (itself a spatial word of aboveness). We look up to some people, and look down upon others. We go up in a class, or a job; our hopes rise; we get on top of our troubles; we take over something we can manage, and then hold it down. It is at least arguable that this is so deeply built into us as human beings that kneeling, for example, is self-explanatory. Less clear is whether kissing is similarly self-explanatory, as Europeans might think, or is it culturally conditioned in different societies, so that other ways of showing affection outstrip (and even disqualify) kissing in other cultures?

In a world of fluid congregations, where we want to make visitors welcome the first time they worship with us, where people of different cultural backgrounds regularly mingle, how often do we need to add words of explanation to the ceremonies that we take for granted?

> Music has similar dynamics – I can be moved by Handel's music of 'I know that my redeemer liveth' even without a soloist, but I am so moved *because I already know the words, the meaning*.

Is your worship sacramental?

You may answer with a quick affirmative, if the dominical sacraments are used in your worship. But can your worship as a whole be seen as 'an effectual sign' of God's grace? Does the Holy Spirit work through your worship to 'quicken' the faith of the participants? Is your worship a witness to the wider world, a gateway for the Holy Spirit to transform the community around you?

TO THINK ABOUT

- Look at your building, your furniture, your art and your architecture; look at your sacraments and the provision for them; look at your arranging of people and their use of their bodies and bodily actions.
- How can you make every feature of the physical world which is integral to your worship serve the overall purpose of making the word of God powerful in people's lives, bringing them into a closer walk with God and with each other?

More on this in chapters D1 To Become More Like Jesus and D2 Crossing Thresholds.

C2

BAPTISMAL

Baptism – enjoined by Jesus

Baptism was part of Jesus' 'Great Commission', obeyed by the apostles and those who came after them. As a ceremony commanded by Jesus it is recognized by the Church of England as one of the 'sacraments of our Lord', a rite with an outward and visible sign and an inward and invisible grace. The twenty-first-century Church of England claims that well over 20 million people in England today have been baptized by it, and are arguably members of it.

> Go therefore and make disciples of all nations, baptizing them in the name of the Father and of the Son and of the Holy Spirit, and teaching them to obey everything that I have commanded you. (Matt. 28.19–20)

The number of infants baptized by the Church of England has been declining, year on year, for several decades, but the Church has recently launched the 'Christenings Project' to turn around that decline. We will return later to the challenges that this poses for parishes which want to make use of this opportunity to engage with a new generation, without devaluing the sacrament.

Meaning – and efficacy

How then does baptism appear in scripture? There is no treatise on it, no chapter of Paul's letters given to expounding its meaning. Instead it is taken for granted as accompanying, and in some sense inaugurating, individuals' Christian lives. Thus it appears, not only within the Great Commission, but also in the nine separate accounts of the actual giving of baptism in the Acts of the Apostles. Thus too Paul mentions it at intervals in his epistles, not in order to dwell on it or expound its meaning, but taking it for granted as a given point of entry upon the Christian landscape, and using it in passing as a point of reference for those traversing the territory. Taking Acts and Paul together, these varied passing references express a great range of meanings, among which we may note:

- repentance and faith (Acts 2.38);
- gifts of the Spirit (Acts 2.38; 10.44–47);
- washing away of sins (Acts 22.16);
- coming under Christ's headship (1 Cor. 1.13);
- union with Christ in his death and resurrection (Rom. 6.3–4);
- incorporation into the body of Christ (1 Cor. 12.13);
- becoming one with all other believers (Eph. 4.5);
- putting on Christ as a garment (Gal. 3.27);
- being adopted as a child of God (Gal. 3.26–27);
- walking in 'newness of life' (Rom. 6.3–4);
- inheriting the final resurrection (1 Cor. 15.29).

The overall implication is that all that is involved in becoming a disciple is represented and signified in baptism – and the appeal that Paul then makes to baptism is not a call to his readers to cast their minds back to remember the actual occasion of their baptism, but to understand *here and now* what it is to be baptized disciples. Baptism has conferred a status, and Paul appeals to that given status – treating baptism as a given fact in their lives, and using it as a fulcrum on which to place the lever of the word to move them on in their Christian lives.

 The language used about baptism in the New Testament normally states it actually effects what it signifies. In the Great Commission, for instance, giving baptism is part of making people disciples; the outward sign and the inward meaning are bound together. Nevertheless there are untidy examples where the outward and inward have come apart:

- in Acts 8 the Samaritans were baptized (8.4), but only received the Spirit later (8.14–17);
- in Acts 10 the Gentile converts received the Spirit first, and were then baptized, with Peter expressing a surprised sense of having to catch up with the work of the Spirit;
- and in 1 Corinthians 10.1–4 the Corinthians are warned, from the example of the Israelites of old, that being baptized (and indeed communicant) is no automatic guarantee of God's favour if lives are not conformed to the significance of the baptism.

The generally serene acceptance in the New Testament that baptism has effected what it signifies is undergirded by the apostolic practice of baptizing within minutes of their hearers turning to Christ. Thus people's Christian lives could be traced back unreflectively to either their conversion or their baptism – conversion and baptism were normally treated then as one event, whatever logical knife–edge we would nowadays wish to insert between them.

Other baptismal questions

History and experience, against the above biblical background, have bequeathed us the following further pressing questions:

Who should be the minister of baptism?

In the Great Commission, 'baptize' is used in the active – the evangelists are themselves to baptize. But in Acts and in Paul the verb is almost always in the passive, the major exceptions being in Acts 8.38 (where no other Christians but Philip were present) and in 1 Corinthians 1.13–17 (where Paul is saying that, although he had baptized a few people, his task was to preach the word, not to administer the baptisms). So, in the last analysis, a baptism given by a lay person is perfectly valid, but understandably the churches have generally viewed baptism as a ministerial function, ministers being ordained to minister the sacraments.

How should baptism be ministered?

We do not know whether in the New Testament converts were being submerged, or whether water was poured upon them. Submersion has had its advocates down history (not least in the Baptist Churches), with the advocacy often based upon the symbolism of death and resurrection from Romans 6.3–4. However, as shown above, there is a great variety of symbolism attaching to baptism, and, however desirable submersion may seem to some, the definition of a sacrament cannot depend on our ability in some way to dramatize its symbolism, let alone one specific symbolic act. The Church of England orders 'dipping' as the first option, 'pouring' as the fall-back. Sprinkling or smearing may be needed in some extreme cases (e.g. for someone in intensive care), and, so long as water touches the candidate, would be valid, but 'irregular'.[93]

> We have been buried with him by baptism into death, so that, just as Christ was raised from the dead by the glory of the Father, so we too might walk in newness of life. (Rom. 6.4)

How can submersion be administered? Most church buildings are not equipped with a tank, but the rubric still says candidates can be dipped. Temporary facilities can be found where there is a will to do so: inflatable paddling pools, builders' tanks, or (appropriately!) hired birthing pools. In some places a procession to the sea or a lake or river is possible – or a local swimming-pool may be hired. Borrowing a local Baptist church and its facilities is not recommended – it gives a strong message that the Church of England really does not offer submersion!

---

93 'The minister dips each candidate in water, or pours water on them.' CW *Baptism Service*.

Along with the water should come words, for which the trinitarian phrasing from the Great Commission has become the regular universal form; and it is pointless to look for other terminology. It has also become widespread use to pour water three times as each Person of the Trinity is named, and Anglicans using submersion have also generally used this triple administration.

Should infants be baptized?

Clearly, they *are* baptized, but are we right to do it? It has been easy over the past 450 years for gospel Christians to say 'Baptism requires expressed repentance and faith, and an infant cannot express them, therefore an infant cannot be baptized – and those who purport to baptize infants are deceiving them and their families'. A full defence of infant baptism against this sweeping one-line elimination takes time.[94] But 'households' figure strongly in the baptisms recorded in the New Testament, and Paul's letters, as indicated above, treat all those to whom they are addressed as baptized, and those recipients included children.[95]

However, any biblical rationale for baptizing infants will depend upon the parents being themselves believers; and thus, when parents with little understanding of the faith of Christ and no practice of Christian worship ask for baptism for their infant, the Church is placed in a difficult position.

How does confirmation relate to baptism?

Confirmation is not found in the Bible, and is not a sacrament commanded by Christ. As a practice of the early Church re-created by the Anglican reformers it is the occasion for those baptized as infants to ratify publicly at an age of discretion the baptismal vows that had been made in their name when they were infants. It has (rightly) ceased to be the exclusive qualification

---

94 See Colin Buchanan, *A Case for Infant Baptism*, GBW 20 revised edition, 2009.

95 Household baptisms: Acts 10.24, 48, Acts 16.15, Acts 16.33, 1 Cor. 1.16. Compare these verses in the letter to child and adult Christians in Colossae: 1.1, 3.20, 2.11–12, 2.20.

for admission to Communion, as baptism stands out as complete sacramental initiation, and visitors and children below the age for confirmation are admitted on the basis of their baptism. Formally, some parishes still expect confirmation before admission to Holy Communion, and confirmation remains canonically required for candidates for ordination and for lay persons being elected to diocesan synods or to General Synod.

Confirmation has a number of pastoral virtues in common with adult baptism:

- the preparation is an opportunity for intensive teaching and building relationships;
- the event itself is a public witness, important for the growth of the candidate, and sowing seeds among their family and friends;
- candidates can be challenged to live as disciples in the world and as active members of Christ's body.[96]

When an adult is baptized, it is arguable that there remains little point in being confirmed as well, but the Church of England's system still currently requires it, and the CW provision rather expects the baptism and confirmation to be ministered within the same rite. The bishop is a visible symbol of the local church's connection with the worldwide Church. (See A1 Relational.)

Baptismal services

The Church of England has always had officially authorized forms of service, and ministers are required to use only those forms. The 1662 BCP had separate services for those baptized as adults and those baptized as infants. However, not only is there today an occasional 'household' where parents and children are baptized together, but having a single adaptable rite in our modern services ensures that theologically a single story is being held together and told together from it.

---

96 For a Roman Catholic view of the personal significance of baptism and confirmation, see Timothy Radcliffe, *Taking the Plunge: Living Baptism and Confirmation*, Bloomsbury, 2012.

It should go without saying that a service which brings visitors into the church, especially visitors who are not (yet) Christians, should incorporate as far as possible all the best practice commended elsewhere in this book. May your guests be welcomed, edified and wow-ed by all that they experience. May they want to come again! The canonical expectation is that it should come within a main service of a Sunday. If for any reason that is not practical, let there be members of the regular congregation present when the baptism does happen, and require the baptismal family to attend a main service to be welcomed and to be given a certificate.

The service has a number of stages:

- a ministry of the word, which explains some aspect of the meaning of baptism, and the commitment being made today;
- when there are infant candidates, some questioning of their parents and godparents to establish that they are ready to take on the task ahead;
- once the key people have gone to the tank or bath or font, there is prayer over the water for the actual benefits of the baptism;
- then affirmations of the candidates' repentance and faith, perhaps combined with testimony by adults, and expressed by proxy for infants;
- the baptism should have plenty of water visible, with adults encouraged to choose submersion; and after baptism there should be acclamations of joy and a glad welcome into the life of the people of God.[97]

A mandatory secondary ceremony to explain the significance of baptism (not to 'complete' it or add to it) is marking the candidate with the sign of the cross. Optional secondary ceremonies include giving a candle and vesting in a new garment, but multiplying secondary ceremonies can all too easily obscure the

---

97 For a fuller treatment of the baptism service, see Mark Earey, Trevor Lloyd and Ian Tarrant (eds), *Connecting with Baptism*, Church House Publishing, 2007.

centrality of the actual baptism in water. The 'Notes' in CW permit the use of oil along with giving the sign of the cross, but again this adds further layers of meaning which may compete with the core understanding of the baptism.[98]

Rites surrounding baptism

Thanksgiving for the Gift of a Child

Common Worship provides a simple service of thanksgiving for the gift of a child (whether by birth or adoption). The key to it is simply thanksgiving. It is clearly non-sacramental, and it involves no undertakings with respect to the future; and in principle it can be, and is, used for the children of couples or single parents who do not wish to make a serious Christian commitment, but think some Christian service is appropriate. The fact that it is not baptism, nor a sacrament, nor initiatory in any sense, needs to be clearly articulated. It may also be used as a preliminary to baptism, for example when an infant is first brought to church, but before preparations for a baptism have taken place.[99]

Renewal of baptismal vows

The practice of confirming young people when they were sometimes too young to take responsibility for their own discipleship was one of the factors pointing to a need for a public renewal of baptismal vows as a rite which is not confirmation, though it may include a reminder of the meaning of baptism by some sprinkling of the candidates with water. Sometimes those who were baptized by pouring as infants wish in later life to have the experience of submersion; and, just as the profession of faith which was not made by the candidates personally at their baptism can be added when they are of age, so it is not inimical to the once-for-all-for-life nature of baptism to provide the

---

98 See 'Notes', CWCI, pp. 100–1.

99 Does your parish have a thought-through clear policy for dealing with baptism requests? See Connecting with Baptism for some approaches to formulating a policy.

experience of submersion for those who want the symbol of total swamping and commitment. This can very meaningful, a time of true renewal of discipleship of Christ, so long as they confess they come as truly baptized in their infancy now to add this extra dimension, with the renewal of vows, to that baptism already given.[100]

Between catacombs and Christendom

At times in its first few centuries, the church in Rome met underground in the catacombs, for fear of persecution; in more recent centuries in other countries the Church has been a quasi-secret society for the same reason. Yet for many years in England and elsewhere, it has been assumed that everyone is a Christian.

For members of a catacomb church, getting baptized, or having your children baptized, was to risk death. For members of Christendom society, avoiding baptism was considered odd at best, treasonous at worst.

Where are we now? In some parts of English society, the Christian faith is still the assumed norm, in others Christianity is viewed with suspicion; in others, Christianity is just one option from a large catalogue.

The Church of England's Christening Project is working with a Christendom model. The word 'christening' was chosen because it is the word most used by those asking for what the Bible and *Common Worship* call baptism. The decision was taken to engage with enquirers in the language they use – though the word 'baptism' is still being used for the heart of the ceremony.

'You're the sixth person I've called and all the others only did baptisms' (Quoted by *The Christenings Project*)

---

100 *Common Worship* makes a distinction between *Reaffirmation of Baptismal Vows* which is a ceremony for the whole congregation, perhaps at Easter, or New Year, and *Renewal of Baptismal Vows*, for individuals marking a milestone in their spiritual journey.

In the same way, the *Additional texts for holy baptism,* authorized in 2015 in response to a request from Liverpool clergy, are an attempt to meet people where they are, by using language easier for the visitor to church to follow.[101]

While the Christendom model is still operating in parts of modern society, we have opportunities to share the good news of God's love with families who turn to the church. However, a completely open-door approach lacks continuity with the biblical origins of baptism outlined above, in a world where following Jesus is becoming an ever more counter-cultural choice.

> You do not have to be married or have been a regular churchgoer – as a parent, you do not even have to have been baptized yourself – though you could be.[102]

Cheap christenings may give satisfying short-term statistics, but will be a flawed foundation for the future of the Church.

A church that values baptism should:

- signal up-front (before fixing a date) that baptism is a life-shaping choice;
- prepare parents (and if possible, godparents), perhaps using some of the material from 'Rites on the way' in *Common Worship Christian Initiation*;
- follow up the baptism with whatever means the church has at its disposal.[103]

Baptism undergirding the Christian life

We have seen that Paul regularly refers his readers to the meaning of their own baptism, to remind them they are united with Christ in death and resurrection, are partakers of the Holy Spirit, are members of the body of Christ, and are to walk in the resurrection life

---

101 See Tim Stratford, *Accessible Baptisms: A Commentary on the Alternative Common Worship Texts,* GBW 226, 2015.

102 *Christenings Project* at churchofenglandchristenings.org.

103 The *Rites on the Way* texts can be found in CWCI, pp. 29–50.

of Christ. Apart from actual baptismal occasions, there is little in Anglican liturgy and less in the average round of songs and hymns to stir people about the meaning of their baptism today. Where baptism is not proclaimed, it is perhaps not well valued. But the scriptures present a pattern of church life in which the consciousness of baptism greatly outstripped the usual practice of today. How can those today who are baptized into the name of the Father, Son and Holy Spirit recover that way of living?

> We are the body of Christ. In the one Spirit we were all baptized into one body. Let us then pursue all that makes for peace and builds up our common life.[104]

In a modern society where everything is disposable, where homes, careers and even friends change from year to year, awareness of my identity as a baptized member of Christ's universal Church should be like an anchor in a stormy sea, more significant than my nationality, my politics or my sexuality:

- I have made the transition from death to life.
- I am part of the worldwide multiracial multicultural family of Christ.
- I am to be salt and light in the world.
- This is the way I live for the rest of my life.

(For more on this see *Connecting with Baptism*, pp. 2–8.)

TO THINK ABOUT

- How often do you think of yourself as baptized?
- What does being baptized mean to you?
- When you are sharing your own story, do you mention your baptism?

---

104 CW: Introduction to the Peace.

TO DISCUSS

- What is your church policy for dealing with baptism or christening enquiries?
- When was it last reviewed?
- How often are members reminded of their own baptism through your worship?
- How can we use the wealth of material (introductions, collects, intercessions, prefaces, post-Communion prayers) found in the CWCI seasonal pages (pp. 150–65)?
- How does the church continue to care for those who have been baptized, including those whose families are not seen regularly?

FOR THE WIDER CHURCH

- In trying to promote infant baptism, how can the Christenings Project retain a challenge to discipleship and the way of the cross?
- Could the Christenings Project, or another agency, provide an e-learning resource for godparents?

C3

EUCHARISTIC

An observer from Mars would find many aspects of our worship puzzling, but perhaps the most puzzling would be the sharing of bread and wine (or food and drink like them) which is variously called the Eucharist, Holy Communion, the Lord's Supper, or other names according to local tradition.

All four Gospels tell the story of Jesus sharing a Passover meal with his disciples, and all but John relate the institution of this memorial. Paul's account in his first letter to the Corinthian church is thought to have been written before the Gospels.

This is something that we do in *community*, in *obedience* to Jesus, *repenting* of our sins, *remembering and proclaiming* his death for humanity, *accepting* it for ourselves, in a spirit of *thanksgiving*.

> This cup is the new covenant in my blood. Do this, as often as you drink it, in remembrance of me. (1 Cor. 11.25)

Community

The Eucharist was instituted in the context of a communal meal, a Passover feast, and the Church continues to celebrate it in community. Any of us can read the Bible on our own, pray on our own, or sing a hymn on our own, but sharing bread and wine is done as a group activity. It takes two to communicate.

In our Holy Communion, we strengthen our relationship with God, and our relationships as a Christian community. How can the way that we celebrate this feast emphasize its communal aspect? (See A1 Relational.)

Who is here? Experts disagree as to how many people were present at the Last Supper of Jesus – some suggest that there were more than 13. A Passover meal would involve everyone in the household: all generations, including children. Some churches encourage children to receive the sacrament, and the Church of England has procedures for the admission of baptized children to Communion before they are confirmed; other churches invite unconfirmed children for a blessing.[105] (See A2 Caring and Inclusive.)

Some Church of England parishes have been admitting children to Communion before confirmation since the 1980s, with well-articulated theological reasons for doing so – there should be many adults now who can reflect on their experience of receiving Communion in this way, and can help form future policy and practice. Did this help them and their peers to remain active church members through their teenage years? Did it help them to grow in discipleship and witness to others? A recent report, *Rooted in the Church*, encourages admitting children to Communion on grounds of equality and intergenerational integration, but shows no statistics to back up the effectiveness of this.[106]

TO THINK ABOUT

- *Where are we?* Do people sit close together, or scattered far apart? (See A4 Located.)
- With a small congregation it is possible to gather around the table for the Eucharistic Prayer, as a family gathers around its meal table (or did before TV meals reduced the use of dining tables).

---

105 See Canon B15A and the *Admission of Baptised Children to Holy Communion Regulations*, 2006; Trevor Lloyd, *Children at Communion: How to Involve Children in the Eucharist*, GBW 205, 2010; and Peter Reiss, *Infants and Children: Baptism and Communion*, GBW 222, 2015.

106 Church of England Education Office, *Rooted in the Church*, GS2056, 2016.

- Can a congregation be encouraged to sit closer together, and not be scattered throughout a large space? And then, at the time of the distribution, to gather around the table, in a circle or at least a semi-circle, to receive?

In the BCP the words, 'Draw near with faith ...' were originally an invitation to all who were 'minded to receive' Communion to gather around the table.

Neither the practice of receiving kneeling in a line, all facing in the same direction, nor that of queuing to receive standing at a specified reception point, builds the sense of community which should be integral to this experience. Obviously each congregation is constrained by the geography of the building that it inherits, but in the course of time buildings can be adapted and changed, and there is visible evidence of this in many church buildings today, where a table now stands at the head of the nave, instead of, or as well as, against the east wall at the far end of the chancel.

What are we praying? Our Eucharistic Prayers are rich in theology and imagery, which many will best appreciate if they are able to read them with their own eyes – it is good therefore to print or project the full text of the prayer, not only the responses.

Common Worship gives us a limited number of authorized Eucharistic Prayers, but with prayers A, B and E there is permission to rewrite the first part of the prayer, known as the preface. Sam Wells and Abigail Kocher have prepared a book of 150 Eucharistic Prayers carefully authored to complement the readings set in the three-year Revised Common Lectionary: while these might be usable in other denominations, in the Church of England only the prefaces should be used.[107]

107 See Ian Tarrant, *Worship and Freedom in the Church of England – Exploring the Boundaries*, GBW 210, 2012; and Samuel Wells and Abigail Kocher, *Joining the Angels' Song*, Canterbury Press, 2016.

The *Common Worship* Eucharistic Prayers include more words for all to join in than the BCP prayer, and enhance the communal ownership of the prayer. Singing the shared words together enhances the communality, *if* all can join in. A choir singing them on behalf of the congregation, however, is of questionable value, especially if the language used is not known to the congregation.

What do we share? Using bread which is visibly broken in pieces after the Eucharistic Prayer (not diced before the service) reminds us of the body of Jesus 'broken' in sacrifice, and emphasizes *our* sharing in *one* body. Some congregations prefer to use wafers (whether for convenience, or in memory of the unleavened bread of the Passover meal), and for such congregations large wafers can be obtained, scored to break into 16 or more pieces, in preference to using individual wafers.

Would it be possible, and theologically acceptable, to write a metrical Eucharistic Prayer for the whole congregation to sing together?

When he had given thanks, he broke it and said, 'This is my body, which is for you'. (1 Cor. 11.24)

TO DISCUSS

- Are your Eucharists truly community events? How can you make them more so?
- Does your parish (or Fresh Expression of Church) celebrate more than one Eucharist on a Sunday, or in the week, with different people attending? Does this fragment your community?
- How do you ensure strangers who come into your church feel welcome?
- When did you last review your parish policy on the admission of children to Communion? Is it time to reflect again on how you involve children in this service? Can you learn anything from the adults within the church community who were admitted to Communion before confirmation?

Obedience

Jesus said, 'Do this, as often as you drink it ...' The ideal frequency of celebrating the Eucharist has been debated over the centuries, and today there is great local variation in the scheduling of these services – in some worshipping communities, the Eucharist is the norm for the main weekly service, with daily celebrations available too; while at the other extreme it can be a special event once a month or even less often.

Any uncertainty about what this sacrament means, or how we should celebrate it, should not keep us from doing it. This is one of our Lord's last commands to his followers – so let us obey.

> 'Twas God the Word that spake it,
> He took the Bread and brake it:
> And what that Word did make it,
> That I believe and take it.
> (Attributed to Elizabeth I, 1688)

If we cannot obey in such a little thing, how shall we obey in greater things?

This act of obedience can be a sign of our commitment to obey Jesus in our whole lives, even if that obedience takes us to the anguish of Gethsemane or the pain of Calvary. The sacrifice that Jesus made should inspire us to sacrificial service, so that Christians leave the church ready to be 'living sacrifices', as one of the *Common Worship* prayers puts it.

The word 'Mass' used by some Christians to describe the Eucharist derives from the Latin for sending – as the service ends we are sent out to do God's work in the world: 'Go in peace to love and serve the Lord'.

The 2017 report from the Archbishops' Council, *Setting God's People Free* (GS2056) asks the question, 'How does what we do as a church, ordained and lay together, enable God's people to grow in their capacity to live out the Good News of Jesus in all of life – in service in the church and in the world?' (See D3 Worship, Mission and Pastoral Care.)

TO DISCUSS

- Should you review the frequency and timings of eucharistic services in your worshipping community?
- Should there be opportunities for individuals to opt into more Eucharists if they want to?
- How can your worship enhance the imperative to go and serve?

Repenting

'Died he for me, who caused his pain … ?' wrote Wesley. As Christians we need to return to God's mercy again and again, seeking forgiveness of our sins, and resolving to live differently in the future. The Greek word translated 'repent' means a change of mind leading to a change of direction. Our English word comes from a Latin verb, 'to think again'.

The BCP Holy Communion, and to a lesser extent the CW services, have been criticized by some for dwelling too much on sin and repentance. It is argued that people whose self-esteem is already low are not helped by being constantly reminded of their sinfulness. 'Can't we just say "Sorry" at the beginning of the service and leave it at that?' But the theme of sin and forgiveness is integral to the crucifixion and to the Eucharist, so it cannot be swept under the carpet. It is essential however to emphasize the Good News that our sins are forgiven and we can have a new start.

The strife is o'er,
the battle done;
the victory of life is won;
the song of triumph has
begun. Alleluia!
(seventeenth century Latin
hymn, translated by Francis
Pott, 1861)

In the usual structure of a Eucharist we repent of our sins near the beginning of the service. However, it may sometimes be more appropriate to use prayers or rituals of penitence later in the service, after the ministry of the word and the intercessions. Many Anglican liturgies follow this pattern, that of the 1662 BCP, where this invitation is used:

Ye that do truly and earnestly repent of your sins, and are in love and charity with your neighbours, and intend to lead a new life, following the commandments of God, and walking from henceforth in his holy ways; draw near with faith ... and make your humble confession to Almighty God ...[108]

Within CW there are a number of authorized confession texts with different styles and emphases. There is also permission to use penitential sentences before the three petitions of the Kyries. Examples are given, but so is permission to choose one's own penitential sentences. This freedom is much appreciated – but may not work if the sentences reflect neither our sinfulness nor God's holiness.

The words of the *Agnus Dei* (Lamb of God), which may be said or sung just before people receive the bread and wine, are designed to help us take pause and recall the awfulness of sin in the sight of God, and the cost to God of sin's remedy. There is scope here, too, for doing things differently from time to time. If you don't already use these words, try including them occasionally. If the choir sings them the same way every week, how about trying a different setting, or a solo, or a short congregational item, just occasionally? (See C8 Musical.)

Lamb of God,
you take away the sin of the world,
have mercy on us.
Lamb of God,
you take away the sin of the world,
grant us peace.

Common Worship Order One also provides for the congregation to say a Prayer of Humble Access (one of two different versions) just before receiving. Again, the words are powerful – how many congregations never use them? Does it blunt their impact to use them every week? The second form delights in our journey from

---

108 See NPW, section B.

past unworthiness to future sharing in the heavenly banquet.[109] (See D5 Eschatological.)

TO DISCUSS

- How can our Eucharists better encourage deep repentance?
- How often do you use a Prayer of Humble Access? Do you make use of both versions?
- Do we need both a Prayer of Humble Access and the *Agnus Dei* in the same service?

Remembering and proclaiming

Jesus said, 'Do this ... in remembrance of me'. We mark past events in our own lives, the lives of our families, and the lives of our communities, in many different ways. Celebrating a birthday or a wedding anniversary. Remembering the dead of two World Wars and other conflicts. The anniversary of the building or opening of our church. We use words, and symbols and music. We gather, we eat, we drink.

In the Eucharist we remember the death of Jesus, and all its benefits for us. We use challenging words, potent symbols and emotion-rich music. We gather around the table, we eat the bread, we drink the wine.

How can we keep the memory fresh? How do we avoid becoming blasé about what we are doing?

- The cycle of the church year can help us in this, with services on Maundy Thursday and the Day of Thanksgiving for the Institution of Holy Communion (the Thursday after Trinity Sunday), as well as the Lectionary readings providing a different focus from time to time.
- *Common Worship* offers us ten different Eucharistic Prayers, and most of them permit some variations. You can write your

---

109 CW, p. 181; note also a shorter form in the ASB on p. 170.

own prefaces for some of the prayers – don't get stuck in a rut.[110]

- Use diverse and vivid images of the cross – there is a wealth of Christian art, and you can ask members of the church to create their own. Maintain a variety of art and music. (See A3 Creative.)

Paul writes of the Eucharist as a proclamation of the death of Jesus – but surely he is referring not only to the death, but also resurrection from the dead, and the victory over sin. How can something, which many consider intimate and personal, yet be a proclamation?

First, it is a proclamation to those who take part, as explained above, by reminding us of the key role of the death of Jesus in our salvation. John Wesley spoke of Holy Communion as a 'converting ordinance', not so much for its witness to those without faith, but for its power to increase the faith of those with but little faith.

> For as often as you eat this bread and drink the cup, you proclaim the Lord's death until he comes. (1 Cor. 11.26)

Nevertheless, it is also a witness to others, whether they are present to observe, or only hear about the Eucharist second-hand, that the death of Jesus is of primary importance to us. The early Church was misunderstood by some to be practising cannibalism; the modern Church is mocked by atheists for using cannibalistic language. However, rather than refrain from mentioning the Eucharist when sharing our faith with others, perhaps we should have the courage to explain what we do, and say what it means to us? Christians should be taught to speak of the Eucharist with confidence and passion to match their other apologetic.

---

110 The Preface is the part of the Eucharistic Prayer following the opening responses.

In the bread and wine of the Eucharist, as in the sacrament of baptism, the past and future come to meet us in the present.[111]

TO DISCUSS

- How can you use the visual arts to give your congregation a fresh take on the death of Jesus from week to week or season by season? (Your answer may depend on whether you use data projection, your own seasonal booklets, or printed service sheets.)
- Do the musical settings and the repertoire of songs relating to the Eucharist need to be refreshed from time to time?
- Would it help to have a sermon series, or small group study material on the Eucharist?
- How do you explain Holy Communion to the world in your website and other publicity? How can you do this without making it exclusive?

Acceptance

 As the individual Christian receives the bread or the wine, he or she says 'Amen' for himself or herself. This may be the only scripted *solo* utterance of that believer in the service. It is a personal word of faith, underlining their personal acceptance of the physical sign, and the spiritual grace on offer. Receiving the bread and the wine are personal acts, by which each of us welcomes the life of Jesus into our life. We may pray:

So cleanse and feed us
with the precious body and blood of your Son,
that he may live in us and we in him.[112]

---

111 N. T. Wright writing in *Reformed Worship*, 91, March 2009.
112 CW, p. 181, second prayer before the distribution.

This should be the climax of the service for the individual, when grace is received; the moment of closest approach to the divine, in which the relationship with Christ is renewed, from which the journey outward in mission continues. This is when the Holy Spirit should re-fill the believer's heart, and set her or him on fire for the Lord.

> For though he withdrew his flesh from us, and with his body ascended to heaven, he, however, sits at the right hand of the Father; that is, he reigns in power and majesty, and the glory of the Father. This kingdom is not limited by any intervals of space, nor circumscribed by any dimensions. Christ can exert his energy wherever he pleases, in earth and heaven, can manifest his presence by the exercise of his power, can always be present with his people, breathing into them his own life, can live in them, sustain, confirm, and invigorate them, and preserve them safe, just as if he were with them in the body; in fine, can feed them with his own body, communion with which he transfuses into them. After this manner, the body and blood of Christ are exhibited to us in the sacrament.[113]

What can be done to enhance this moment? Most people would prefer any background music to be gentle rather than lively at this point – but personalities differ! Most would prefer not to be hurried out of the way so that the next person can receive, but this often happens with a larger congregation. Somebody being prepared to receive Holy Communion for the first time might be told to come forward to receive, and to stay in that place only until the person next to them has received. (See C8 Musical.)

In a small gathering, where worshippers are positioned in an arc or around a table, it may be possible for the ministers to take the elements to the people where they are sitting or standing – then there is no need to move after receiving. In a larger café church environment this might be reproduced by having people receive at their tables.

---

113 John Calvin (1509–64), *Institutes of the Christian Religion*, 4.17.18.

Sometimes in less formal settings communicants pass the bread and wine from one to another. If people are comfortable with this, it enhances community. However, the imperative to communicate the next person can mar the moment of acceptance, unless the 'backstitch' method is used.

Common Worship offers a choice of words for the distribution of communion: different ones may be used in different circumstances. However, people can find it distracting if ministers use different words with different people in the same service. 'Why did she say that to him, but not to me?'

> 'Backstitch' distribution: person A gives plate to B, who administers bread back to A; B then passes plate on to C, who administers bread back to B; etc.

TO DISCUSS

- What link is there between the individual being accepted by the worshipping community, and the individual accepting the grace of Christ?
- What kind of music, if any, do you prefer while receiving Holy Communion?
- How would you explain to a non-Christian what the Eucharist means to you?

Thanksgiving

The word *Eucharist* comes from the Greek for giving thanks, and the early establishment of this title for the service with bread and wine suggests that thanksgiving may have been the prime focus of the service for the early Christians. We are giving thanks for the death of Jesus on the cross for us, with all that means for our forgiveness and renewed relationship with his Father and ours.

Just as the Passover meal was a celebration and thanksgiving for the liberation of God's people from captivity and oppression in Egypt, our eucharistic meal is a celebration and thanksgiving for our liberation from captivity to sin and the sentence of death. The more seriously we take the consequences of sin, the more heartfelt and the more joyful will be our thanksgiving.

While the Eucharist has its solemn side, it is also an occasion for rejoicing. Party-poppers may be over the top, but light and colour and melody and rhythm are called for! Even if you prefer the music during the distribution to be subdued, the hymn afterwards should, on most occasions, raise the roof. The lost sheep, the lost coin, and the lost son are found! Jesus is risen, and in Christ all have been made alive! Thanks be to God, for he gives us the victory through our Lord Jesus Christ!

Our celebration at the Lord's table looks forward to the banquet foretold in Isaiah 25, and referred to by Jesus in Matthew 8.11. (See D5 Eschatological.)

Some people speak of the person leading the Eucharist as the one who 'celebrates'. However, *all* the worshippers should be celebrating, so it is better to call the leader something else – see A5 Well-led.

TO DISCUSS

- How can you be sure of ending the Eucharist on a note of thanksgiving and praise?
- On what occasions would you *not* want to?

C4

ENCOUNTERING THE
LIVING GOD

 What do we expect people to get out of a church service? Mark Earey produced a grid which analysed the differing way in which different groups of people might experience a church service, one quadrant of which he summarized as the 'wow factor'. This is sens-

Quotes from two different worshippers:

'That choral singing hit me right in the solar plexus!'

'The mid-week Communion is as refreshing as a four-mile run.'

ing the presence of God and encountering God, even if the worshipper cannot articulate this. This 'wow factor' may be immediate, encountering God in one particular act of worship, or long-term, the cumulative effect of sensing God's presence in worship, even if your attendance at worship is sporadic. Thus this applies to regular worshippers and to occasional visitors.[114]

God's own people and their place

The story of the Golden Calf and its follow-up in Exodus 32 and 33 conceal a significant theological theme, helpfully unlocked by theologian Samuel Terrien (1911–2002). After God has punished those responsible for the idolatrous worship of the calf, he calls the Israelite community to continue their journey, and tells them

---

114 Mark Earey and Carolyn Headley, *Mission and Liturgical Worship*, GBW 170, 2002, p. 10.

that he himself will not accompany them, but will instead send an angel to go with them. This news is greeted with dismay by Moses and the community. If you don't go with us, cries Moses, how will anyone know we are your people? What will mark us out as in any way different from everyone else around us? If we lose your presence, we lose all our significance and distinctiveness![115]

Terrien continues to trace this theme of the presence of God among his people and finds it to be a major motif throughout the Old Testament. Perhaps this is most clearly seen in the departure of the 'glory' from the Temple in Ezekiel 10, and its subsequent return in chapter 48, such that the renewed and restored city has as its name 'The Lord is there'. Terrien suggests that the presence of God among his people is the most significant facet of Old Testament theology, and it is of course a theme which continues into the New, signalled by the announcement of the name of the Messiah as 'Emmanuel' – 'God with us', and fulfilled in the final words of Jesus (according to Matthew) 'I am with you always, even to the end of the age'.

This sets apart the Judaeo-Christian faith as a religion of the presence of God. All the competing gods and systems of worship in the Ancient Near East (and indeed to this day) worship a god who is 'up there' or 'out there' or 'over there', a god whom we have to seek and attempt to reach by our own efforts or devotions; followers of Yahweh have a God present among his people. To worship him holds the possibility at least of an encounter with him.

Terrien is, of course, clear in stating that the presence of God does not mean the containing or constraining of God. 'The heavens, even the highest heavens, cannot contain him', prays Solomon, so how much less his house? (We might say 'how much less our worship-service?'). But although the Temple could not contain God, it was the place where his availability was particularly focused. In the same way, Christians believe that God is indeed with them wherever they go and whatever they do. But our periods and places of worship do provide a particular

---

115 Samuel Terrien, *The Elusive Presence,* Harper & Row, 1978.

focus for that presence. As comedian Harry Hill says: 'It's amazing how often, when you're studying ants on a hot summer's day through a magnifying glass, they spontaneously burst into flames!' The light and warmth of the sun is always there, but it may be either obscured by clouds or focused powerfully into a time and place.

> Will God indeed dwell on the earth? Even heaven and the highest heaven cannot contain you, much less this house that I have built! (1 Kings 8.27)

We have already looked at Harold Turner's distinction between seeing our worship space as 'temple', the place where we meet God, and as 'meeting house', where we primarily meet with one another, but hope thereby to encounter God. (See the first part of A4 Located, and the questions there.)

Meeting with God today

All this theology of presence and place suggests that our worship ought to hold at least the possibility of an encounter with the living God who is present among us, and whose presence is particularly focused when we deliberately give ourselves to worshipping him in the community of his people.

> Over 30 years of teaching on worship I usually begin by asking people to identify an occasion when the presence of God was particularly felt, and people rarely come up with anything from their own local church or habitual worship.[116]

Many Christians would be able to remember particular times and places where that sense of encounter was strong, even life-changing. But research suggests that these moments of encounter rarely happen in the context of a regular Sunday service in one's normal church. Rather they are to be found at conferences, festivals, cathedrals or retreats, or out in the countryside.

---

116 Unpublished research by John Leach.

The challenge now is how planners and leaders of worship, as well as participants in it, can recover the expectation that the Lord is here and his Spirit is with us, and that we might actually meet with him in a way which leaves us in no doubt that we have done so. This surely must be a key aim for all our worship.

Rudolf Otto (1869–1937) published his book *The Idea of the Holy* in 1917. This is a study of a particular phenomenon which Otto identified as occurring in most if not all religions, though he does draw extensively on the Bible and Christian faith to make his case. Otto describes what he labels 'the numinous' – an awareness of something beyond human beings and the natural world – which would certainly include Christian awareness of God. This he further describes by the Latin words *mysterium tremendum et fascinans*. We might use Otto's analysis to begin to describe elements of how we encounter God in worship.[117]

Mysterium

While it is tempting to translate this as 'mystery', that might cause more problems than it solves. The reference is really to God as being separate from us: 'wholly other' is a phrase that many writers use. We need look no further than Genesis 1 to see that this is central to biblical faith. God is not the same as a human being and indeed is not part of creation. This crucial difference and distance between humans and God is fundamental to establishing the relationship of worship. We do not worship ourselves, or another part of creation or nature – rather we worship God who is wholly other. A famous classic hymn puts it like this:

> Immortal, invisible, God only wise,
> in light inaccessible hid from our eyes,
> most blessed, most glorious, the ancient of days,
> almighty, victorious, thy great name we praise.

It is not hard to find more modern examples.

---

117 Rudolf Otto, *Das Heilige*, 1917, English translation, Oxford University Press, 1920, also available online at archive.org.

Tremendum

This aspect of Otto's description points to the greatness of God. God is not just wholly other than us but is also great and beyond our complete understanding. Taken together, these words indicate a God who evokes our respect and worship. If we leave it there, we have a remote God with whom we cannot have much contact. If we do not take enough notice of this aspect of God's character, we run the risk of taming and domesticating God.

Fascinans

This is Otto's third word. Faced with the God who is *mysterium tremendum* we might run away and hide. We are so small compared to God's greatness. We are so sinful compared to God's holiness. Yet we do not always run. Often we stay, transfixed by this God. There is just something that means we cannot forget it and go on our way. We must investigate more, or at least stay and soak it in.

Just outside Seattle are the Snoqualmie Falls. As you stand some distance away watching the sheer power of the waterfall, the spray drifts across the valley and you soon get quite wet. On a hot summer's day you can walk away from the edge and soon dry off but you go back because the power of the water is fascinating. The scene draws you back. Likewise with God, we are drawn back – there is just something there that fascinates us. We cannot always describe it or articulate our feelings, but we are drawn back.

Paradoxes of worship

Michael Perry (1933–2015) pointed out that worship involves several paradoxes. One is this:

> Worship is not a human activity directed at God, but a divine activity initiated by God in which we are privileged to share.

God draws men to worship with him; the Father seeks people to worship him in Spirit and in truth.[118]

We will look in greater detail at two more paradoxes.

Transcendence and immanence

While in many faiths worship is addressed to one who is 'wholly other', Christians worship a God who did become one of us in Jesus. We encounter God who is not us but who became one of us. While worship is not the only place where this encounter takes place, it is a key place where this happens.

This is the paradox of transcendence and immanence, which inspires a number of hymns, worship songs and liturgical texts, such as 'King of kings, majesty, God of Heaven living in me'.[119]

Multiplying the names and being silent

Faced with the transcendent God, the *mysterium tremendum*, what are we to do? We worship this God – but how? Words cannot describe God or indicate the totality of his greatness. Two approaches therefore developed in Christian spirituality and worship.

One says that God can be described in an almost limitless number of ways so we need to use as wide a variety of names and descriptions as possible. Denys Turner, formerly Norris-Hulse Professor of Divinity at Cambridge University, calls this approach 'multiplying the names'.[120]

Common Worship is not always very good at doing this. For example, while the Liturgical Commission's own policy document stated that CW would draw on a range of biblical images for God, in fact images of God as father, king and provider predominate. In the CW collects, God is described as 'almighty' in

---

118 Michael Perry, *The Paradox of Worship*, SPCK, 1977.

119 Jarrod Cooper, Sovereign Lifestyle Music, 1996.

120 Denys Turner, *The Darkness of God: Negativity in Christian Mysticism*, Cambridge University Press, 1998; *The Worship of the Church as it Approaches the Third Millennium*, GS Misc 364, 1991.

the opening description in 42 per cent of them. The next highest percentages are 'Eternal' (14 per cent) and 'Lord' (11 per cent). The alternative collects use more diverse imagery, with no one description predominating beyond 'almighty' (now at 13 per cent) and 'Father' (at 11 per cent, up from 9 per cent in the CW original collects). No one is saying that these ways of describing God are not true – it's just that there are so many other things that the Bible says about God that do not feature so often in our worship. Sometimes this approach is therefore called 'expansive language' – expanding our view of God by using lots of biblical descriptions.

Two technical terms: *kataphatic* theology describes from many perspectives what God *is* like (e.g. loving, powerful); while *apophatic* theology speaks of what God *is not* like (e.g. invisible, unhasting).

However, in the end, even lots of words won't fully describe God. Human language cannot do it. So another approach is to say that, faced with this transcendent God, the only appropriate response is silence. We fall silent in worshipful awe in the face of God. This approach too has a technical term: *apophatic* theology. Quaker worship is the supreme example of this with its stress on waiting on God in silence. The balance between transcendence and immanence is matched by balancing apophatic and kataphatic approaches to worship and prayer.

TO DISCUSS

- Analyse the songs and hymns you use. Do they tend towards the transcendent or immanent view of God? Analyse the titles and descriptions of God in your worship. Is God always called holy, mighty, father, king and so forth? How often is God merciful, loving, generous or suffering? How could you monitor this long-term?
- Do the same for preaching and praying – what images of God predominate?
- Is your worship more kataphatic or apophatic? Remember that both kataphatic and apophatic approaches can mediate both immanence and transcendence.

Meeting with God in our worship

In worship, we may get a sense of God being near – though we may not call it that. There is something we struggle to identify that was special. It might be a phrase in the prayers or hymns. Perhaps it is a ritual act that moves us – when the vicar pours the water over the baby at a baptism for example. Often it is an undefinable atmosphere that is more than just a congregation being welcoming (though that is important!). Something makes a visitor think, 'I might just come back another time'. If that happens most times a person visits a church, there is the 'long-term wow' which Earey describes.

Does *Common Worship* help with this? It is significant that the production of the CW corpus coincided with the peaking of the Charismatic Movement, when many of its insights ceased to be topics of hot controversy and had flowed into the mainstream of the life of the Church. So some kind of prayer ministry, for example, became common across the spectrum of churchmanships. But more subtly a sense crept into the liturgy that worship really should be 'joy' as well as 'duty'. There was a growing recognition that texts, the stock in trade of liturgists, were not in themselves worship, but were only tools to facilitate worship. There is also a growing sense in rubrics and introductory notes that worship might happen as it were *between* the texts: there was a new emphasis on silence, action, movement and gesture, the symbolic, and the physical setting of the liturgy. Typical of this move would be the introduction to the 'Service of the Word':

> Leading people in worship is leading people into mystery, into the unknown and yet the familiar. This spiritual activity is much more than getting the words or the sections in the right order. The primary object in the careful planning and leading of the service is the spiritual direction which enables the whole congregation to come into the presence of God to give him glory.

This is subtle, perhaps for many a relatively new emphasis, and one which CW seems wholeheartedly to endorse.

However, at the end of the day *Common Worship* is a series of texts, and while *New Patterns for Worship*, for example, encourages good practice, some may feel that creativity needs more encouragement than it actually receives. There are many books which seek to resource creativity in worship, which hopefully leads to the possibility of an encounter with God, but very little official material. And of course enabling the encounter with God is only the start: what, as leaders of worship, do we feel the nature of that encounter might be, and how might we help people respond appropriately to it? In some churches prayer ministry 'for anything the Lord has put his finger on for you today' would be *de rigueur*, but CW, while it provides texts for healing prayer, gives little guidance for a well-organized and sympathetic response to the God who may encounter us in worship. (See A3 Creative.)

John Leach's *Responding to Preaching* attempts a modest nod in this direction, but perhaps a fuller and more official exploration of this subject would be a useful addition to the CW corpus.[121]

How can leaders help?

Those leading worship have three tasks: to *expect* God to be present among the worshippers, to use texts and other liturgical resources to *maximize* that possibility, and helpfully to provide opportunities for people to *respond*. To see leading worship as taking the congregation on a route march from the welcome to the blessing is to miss the point. In one church, for example, the text

The Lord is here.
His Spirit is with us.

was regularly followed by a brief period of silence during which people were encouraged to 'tune in' to the presence of the Spirit. (See A5 Well-led.)

---

121 John Leach, *Responding to Preaching*, GBW 139, 1997.

Taking a pause in a conference lecture, or in the midst of a busy day, one may feel the presence of the Spirit powerfully – but it is necessary to stop and allow him space. This is an example of worship-leading which 'allows the text to become reality'. Effective leaders of worship will read the texts looking closely at what they actually say, and helping the meaning of the words to become effective, rather than simply skipping past them and on to the next line.

In some congregations the *Sanctus* at the end of Eucharistic Prayer H, which deliberately is not followed by an 'Amen', is used to launch into a more extended period of singing, which celebrates the presence of God among his worshippers. These are little things, and easy to build in to services, but they begin with a mindset which really does believe that God is present with us in ways which mean that we have a living encounter with him. But underneath this desire for the liturgy to facilitate encounter with the God present among us is a key principle which can best be introduced through an excursion into the world of music.

Many people will at some point have experienced 'tingles down the spine' or 'hairs standing up on end' in response to a certain passage of music. Research by John Leach has spelt out the principle of 'expectancy violation' which is often the cause of this kind of *frisson* or physiological thrill. A prime example is Vaughan Williams' 1953 Coronation arrangement of 'All people that on earth do dwell' to 'Old Hundredth'. In the first four verses, although the treatment is slightly different for each verse, the harmonization is the same. But when we come to the final verse the harmonization is different, and the first line ends on an unexpected E major chord rather than the expected G.[122]

To Fa - ther Son and Ho - ly Ghost

122 John Leach, *Music, Emotion and Worship*, unpublished Lambeth Diploma thesis, 1999.

This moment is a powerful one for the tingles, but what is actually happening? The composer has set up the expectation that the word 'Ghost' will be on a G chord; after all that line has ended on G every single time up until now. But then he violates that expectation with the E, and because even non-musicians subconsciously try to fit music into *schemas* or phrases which we understand, its refusal to fit causes the release of endorphins in the bodies of at least some of the hearers.

For expectancy violation to work, three things have to happen: the expectation has to be set up, it has to be violated, but it has to be violated in a way which 'works'. So Vaughan Williams doesn't use different harmony for each of the first four verses, or else the different fifth verse would not be a surprise. And when he does finally change it, he does so in a way which works: the melody note B is in the chord of G, but it is also in the chord of E, so it still fits. To have stuck a random G# chord in would just have sounded daft.

This musical principle can be used liturgically. For example, after a sermon on wholehearted commitment to God, one might normally have ended the service with the prayer which tells God that we offer him our souls and bodies to be a living sacrifice. But to use instead the Methodist Covenant prayer, which has the same sentiments put more clearly and powerfully, would be the equivalent to the E chord replacing the expected G, and would impact the congregation. On the other hand, to end the service with a random collect for the feast of an obscure saint would be the equivalent of the G# – just silly. The art of good liturgical construction is to do something regularly enough that people expect it, and then now and again to do something different. Getting the proportion of 'usual' and 'different' right is a key skill, which can go wrong in both directions. What one might call the BCP approach is to set up plenty of expectation but never ever to do anything different. The utter predictability is what makes it safe, if a little dull and dutiful. But the danger with the pick'n'mix approach of *Common Worship*, or indeed with churches which don't believe in using very much set liturgy at all, is that it is all violation and no expectancy, as every service is unique and different. Neither of these is likely to give anyone tingles anywhere.

Reality check

Of course an emotional *frisson* is not the same as an encounter with God, but they are linked, and at the very least our emotions, which we so often keep locked down tightly, can, if released, encourage us to know God with us experientially. It would be helpful if this principle were taught and encouraged widely among those planning and leading worship.

Why is encounter important? Because to meet God, now as in biblical times, is to change. Many stories of significant personal encounters with God show that they led to new directions, deeper faith, more committed discipleship, some area of healing or freedom, or a new calling or vocation. We do not have the space to explore a theology of God as the disturber, but many will testify to years of dutiful, faithful worship which one day 'came alive' as something helped them to encounter God – perhaps, in their words, 'for the first time'. How tragic that this can be the case, that we can worship for years without meeting God, and how tragic that while liturgists provide us with more and more texts, leaders often do not know how to use them skilfully in such a way that people's lives are changed. Perhaps we need a moratorium on new words, and a major emphasis on learning how to use the ones we already have.

This encounter with God can happen in any style of worship or in any type of church. It is not about a dramatic event that comes out of the blue (though it can be). It can often be an undefinable atmosphere – a sense that God is here.

TO DISCUSS

• Is the space in which you worship designed for people to meet with God, or to meet with one another? What does it say about the nature of God?

- Does silence ever get much space in your worship? What about music without words as a vehicle for encountering God? Do you ever have a verse or two where the musicians play but there is no singing?
- How can worship be led in such a way that people might actually meet God? An easy way into this question is to reverse it. How can we make it hard for people to meet God? Little things can do this – feedback on the PA, cold buildings that make us uncomfortable, leading the service in a voice that lacks variety in pitch or is just inaudible. Removing the barriers to people meeting God would be a good start.

C5

INTERCESSORY

A young man recently visited Belfast for the first time in his life. His new wife had studied there, and he had heard about it but never visited. He came home full of it: what a beautiful city it was, what a great place in which to live ... And then he admitted 'When we used to pray week after week after week in church for Northern Ireland all those years I was growing up, I used to think "Oh no, not that again! Nothing will ever change". But it has!' Archbishop Desmond Tutu was heard to give the clergy of one English diocese a right telling off: 'Your prayers changed South Africa! They really did! But you don't believe it. You're too faithless!'

Intercessions during worship can be one of the most unreal, and yet the most real, sections of our services. We know the experience of hearing the same old subjects trotted out again and again: Northern Ireland, South Africa, Syria, Iraq ... not to mention that long list of ill people who only seem to move anywhere at all when they get swapped to the bereavement list. And although with hindsight it is sometimes possible to see change as having happened, at the time it can feel thankless, unsatisfying, and simply a waste of breath. We live in a society which expects instant results: a few years ago aspirins were sold not on how effectively they took pain away, but how quickly. At the same time Access credit cards took 'the waiting

> *Contrast:*
> 'We pray yet again for the Middle East'
> *with*
> 'As the widow persisted with the unjust judge, so we persevere in asking you to bring peace and reconciliation to Israel and Palestine'.

out of wanting'. Now if a website doesn't respond to us in a frac-
tion of a second we'll go somewhere else. Intercession reminds us
that God's timing is not the same as ours. 'If it lingers, wait for it'
said God to the prophet (Hab. 2.3). Jesus taught that persistence
in prayer is good for us (Luke 18.1), and the book of Daniel
reminds us of the spiritual battle of which prayer is a part (Dan.
10.13). To build intercession into our worship not only changes
situations in ways which at the time we may not be able to see at
all, but it also builds into Christians a sense of perspective as our
'Now!' worldview is subverted.

The imperative to pray

How will the church of the future pray? First, it *will* pray. In
churches where worship-songs, and lots of them, rule, intercession is one of the first things to go out of the window, or at
best be reduced to a few quick sentences (the second is often the
reading of the Bible, both of which are pretty paradoxical in
evangelical churches). The church will rediscover, if it has lost
it, its priestly role of crying out to God for a world for which
there is no hope without his action, and will give time, effort and
creativity to intercession.

In doing so it will be obedient to the scriptural example of
Jesus, who prayed 'your will be done on earth as it is in heaven',
and in the injunction of Paul to Timothy, urging prayers for all
kinds of people.

Intercessory prayer can be hard work – requiring patience,
research and understanding. But the road of Christian discipleship is not advertised as easy!

> First of all, then, I urge you to offer to God petitions, prayers,
> intercessions, and expressions of thanks for all people, for
> kings, and for everyone who has authority, so that we might
> lead a quiet and peaceful life with all godliness and dignity.
> (1 Tim. 2.1–2)

Honesty

The church will pray honestly. The intercessions, which by their nature focus on the nasty things of life, the problem areas and the heartaches, are probably the part of the service which most closely connects to the real lives of the congregation as they struggle with illness, bereavement, anxiety and all the other ills of life. We have the chance to give voice to the things which really concern us: far more, if we're honest, than the atonement theology of the Eucharistic Prayer or the often shallow words of the Peace. This is so much worse in churches where we are all supposed to be walking in faith and victory all the time, and feel guilty failures if things are not going swimmingly.

The intercessions also connect with the harshness of the world beyond our local community – persecution, exploitation, abuse, starvation and homelessness. You may have links with mission organizations working in situations very different from your own, and which feed back information which can fuel your prayers. If you can take the time to tell those at the front line that you are indeed praying for them, they will be much encouraged.

Contrast:
'We just want to praise your name for our victory over sin'
with
'Thank you for your victory over sin: give us pure hearts, and help us resist temptation'.

Balance

The church will pray in a balanced way. The suggested areas for prayer in the CW Order One Eucharist give us a helpful progression from the church to the world to our local community to those in particular need, ending with an eschatological reminder of our place in the community of saints. So often prayers have never gone wider than the four walls of the church building, and petty internal affairs seem to be all that God is invited to take an interest in.[123]

Common Worship Daily Prayer suggests a number of topics for different days of the week and for the seasons of the church's year – but the topics listed may, of course, be taken into your intercessions at other times too.[124]

Alternative topics will come through the media and the networks to which members of the church belong. All of God's creation is of interest to him. Don't forget those who are often overlooked. Include cleaners as well as bishops, porters as well as doctors and nurses, translators as well as authors, drivers as well as farmers, volunteers as well as employees. Is there anyone in the congregation whose job has never been mentioned? Is there anyone whose home country has never been mentioned?

While the *Common Worship* corpus (including *New Patterns for Worship* and *Times and Seasons*) includes many texts which may be used (perhaps with adaptation) by local congregations, there are many other resources on which you can draw, including other provinces of the Anglican communion, other denominations, and ecumenical sources such as Taizé and Iona.

Contrast:
'Lead our government to repent of its current economic policy.'
with
'May all our politicians remember that one day they will give an account to you'.

Another kind of balance respects the different theological and ideological views within the congregation – the intercessions should not be a mini-sermon or a political manifesto!

Specific

The church will pray specifically. While some have an aversion to 'telling God what to do', avoid the blandness of 'We pray for Africa', or even, as heard on one occasion, 'We pray for the human race'. We may not know the best solution to a complex

---

123 CW lists topics on p. 174, elaborated as a prayer on p. 281.
124 CWDP, pp. 362–5.

international dispute, but we can at least ask God to bring peace and justice to it. We may be concerned for the whole of a certain continent – but it adds focus to name a country which has been in the news recently. We may be anxious for all children taking exams this month – but let's name the school in our parish.

Prayer in scripture is honest and specific, and it seems that we ought to be able actually to tell whether or not it has been answered. Vague prayers don't allow us this luxury, but they do protect us from the awkwardness of failure.

> *Contrast:*
> 'Bless all the dear children in your tender care'
> *with*
> 'Keep safe all the children in our parish, especially those in one-parent households'.

From the heart – and with imagination

The church will pray from the heart of its people. Liturgically speaking intercessions are the most deregulated parts of the provision: although there are many resources available, there is little which is set and immovable, particularly when compared with the approach of the BCP. It is the part of the service, after the readings, which is most likely to be led by a rota of lay people. But in spite of that the subjects for prayer are usually chosen for the congregation by someone else. It ought to be possible to allow the real concerns of the congregation to be featured in prayer. The service leader might ask people to share areas of concern, and then articulate these into prayers; perhaps grouped under the general headings above.

People might be invited to active prayer, lighting candles, sticking post-it notes, using pebbles, blowing bubbles, or releasing balloons, with or without verbal prayers being articulated. This section of the service might be 'liquefied', with different prayer activities available in different areas of the liturgical space around which people can move in their own time. People might be asked to form small groups and pray together (with the get-out clause for nervous visitors, of course, that you can 'just sit and pray quietly on your own if you'd prefer'. There are so many possibilities for this 'democratizing' of intercession which will allow people to experience prayer as something in which they are involved, rather than something to which they sit (or kneel) and listen.[125]

Earnest and expectant

The church will be hopeful and expectant. However you might interpret the theology of chapters 9 to 11 of Romans, there is no mistaking Paul's zealous prayer for his people.

> I have great sorrow and unceasing anguish in my heart ... Brothers and sisters, my heart's desire and prayer to God for them is that they may be saved. (Rom. 9.2; 10.1)

Desmond Tutu had to rebuke the English church for its faithlessness. If only we could plan and lead prayers as though they were an amazing opportunity literally to change the world, maybe our faith would rise and we really would see darkness pushed back and the kingdom of God coming closer. The intercessions ought to be just about the most exciting part of the service.

TO DISCUSS

- Are the whole people of God engaged in the intercessions? Is the congregation ever given an opportunity to suggest topics for prayer? If there is a team of leaders, is it representative of the whole congregation?
- Do those who lead intercessions make use of a wide range of resources?

---

125 See Anna de Lange and Liz Simpson, *How to Lead the Prayers: A Training Course,* GBW 169, 2003. For more detailed reflection and guidance for good practice, see also Sam Wells, *Crafting Prayers for Public Worship,* Canterbury Press, 2013.

- Do you ever celebrate answered prayer?
- How do you handle prayers not being answered in the way you hope for (2 Cor. 12.7–10)?
- If there is a team of intercession-leaders, do they come together to reflect on good practice?

C6

SEEKING WHOLENESS

Basil the Great (329–379) was Bishop of Caesarea in Cappadocia at the time of a plague in 369. His response was to open the basilica to the victims, which led to the founding of a 300-bed hospital, and a range of other buildings including hospices for the poor, aged and dying, wards for sick travellers and a leprosy house. This practical outworking of what happens when Christian faith, ethics, vision and generosity come face to face with the needs of a sick community is echoed down the years in the rule of St Benedict[126] (he has a chapter on caring for the sick), the establishment of hospitals and infirmaries as part of the monastic movement (look at the names of our great teaching hospitals) and the way Christians have often been at the forefront of research and developments in medicine.

> Basil's eucharistic liturgy is still in occasional use in the Eastern Orthodox Church and is the main influence on Eucharistic Prayer F in CW Order One.

Healing and praying, faith and wholeness go hand in hand. All are intimately bound together, and this should not surprise us when we see it happening either in history or in the way God works in the church today, because it is precisely what we find in the ministry of Jesus.

---

126 Benedict (c. 480–543?) was the founder of Western monasticism.

Background

We take a look at a series of stories in Luke's Gospel. In Luke 5.12–25 we find Jesus cleansing a leper and healing a paralytic; in 6.6–19 we see him healing a man with a withered hand and teaching and healing a crowd; in 7.1–17 he heals a centurion's servant and raises the son of a widow from the dead. In chapter after chapter we observe Jesus' desire for people to be made whole, the ministry of others in the community bringing people to Jesus, the need for some expectation and faith, the importance of touch, the command to check things out with the medical authorities. We find the Greek word used most often about physical healing implies wholeness in every way: 'Your faith has saved you' (17.19, 18.42) are his words to the woman with the haemorrhage and to blind Bartimaeus. What is happening is part of the incarnation, bringing God the healer (Ex. 15.26) into the situation, part of establishing the kingdom.

> If you will listen carefully to the voice of the Lord your God, and do what is right in his sight, and give heed to his commandments and keep all his statutes, I will not bring upon you any of the diseases that I brought upon the Egyptians; for I am the Lord who heals you. (Ex. 15.26)

Sin and sickness are sometimes but not always linked. When asked whether a man's blindness is the result of his own sin or that of his parents, Jesus replies, 'Neither' (John 9.2–3); but having healed another man at the pool of Bethesda, he warns him to sin no more or something worse might happen (John 5.14). Healing the sick and casting out unclean spirits are usually separate activities in the ministry of Jesus – and yet occasionally an illness is attributed to a demon, for example the mute man in Matthew 9 and the man both blind and mute in Matthew 12.

The early Church seems to have maintained the expectation of continuing the healing ministry of Jesus. James gives very clear instructions (James 5.14–17) about the sick sending for the elders who will 'rub oil on them in the name of the Lord'. As in the Gospels, this is a holistic ministry, involving confession of sin, and forgiveness, salvation and resurrection. This is the kind of pattern to which many in the Church would like to return. Why is there not more encouragement in this direction? Why did General Synod refuse for years to approve a successor to the 1662 service for the Visitation of the Sick? And why is the provision in CW so restrained and under-exuberant?

History

A bit of potted history might help. In the early Middle Ages we find the sick self-administering Communion and anointing from supplies taken to their homes. This freedom of local ministry was reined in by the church, with stipulations about priests being the only ones to minister in this way. And it was clearly open to abuse and superstition, denounced and outlawed by reformers such as Bucer and Calvin. This and the later medieval focus on preparation for death rather than healing for life led to the BCP service for the Visitation of the Sick continuing in the same direction, but without the anointing and prayer for departure of Extreme Unction.

> The Bible does not make the distinction that we might make today, between sickness and disability.

Once the Tractarian Movement in the nineteenth century began to reintroduce not only the use of oil, but also individual auricular confession, as a prerequisite for absolution, discussion about healing was caught up in the controversies of the Reformation – and divisive debates continued right through to 1982, when liturgy for the sick was finally approved, though without the disputed BCP private absolution ('I absolve you ...') or any provision for blessing oil.[127]

This in part explains the very restrained approach of the CW services. On the positive side, organizations such as the Guild of Health (founded in 1904), the Guild of St Raphael, the Divine Healing Mission and the Dorothy Kerin Trust worked 'to restore

---

127 *Ministry to the Sick* was authorized by Synod in November 1982, for use from June 1983.

the healing ministry of Christ in and through his church' – the aim of the Guild of Health. Charles Gusmer has traced the increasingly positive tone of Lambeth resolutions, as well as the influence of other churches: 'the ministry of healing is not the exclusive concern of sects such as Pentecostalism, Spiritualism and Christian Science, but is an integral part of the mission committed to the whole church by her founder: to preach the Kingdom and to heal the sick'. The Charismatic Movement, noticeable in mainstream denominations of the Church from the 1960s, brought a new enthusiasm for prayer for healing.[128]

Archbishop Lang (*Divine Healing. its Place in the Normal Ministry of the Church of England,* address in 1926 on the twenty-first anniversary of the founding of Guild of St Raphael), pointed to four features of the ministry of healing: intercession, absolution, unction and the laying on of hands, the sacrament of Holy Communion.

Common Worship

In CW *Pastoral Services*, the *Theological Introduction* – and indeed the very title of *Wholeness and Healing* (note the order) – places healing in the wider context of 'human vulnerability and weakness in the face of the dominion of sin and death' and of 'the broader salvation that Jesus brings'. And it is because of this perceived integration of wholeness and healing with salvation that it is to be seen as central to the message of the gospel and therefore central to what the church does when it meets. 'Healing, reconciliation and restoration are integral to the good news of Jesus Christ. For this reason prayer for individuals, focused through laying on of hands or anointing with oil, has a proper place within the public prayer of the church. God's gracious activity of healing is to be seen both as part of the proclaiming of the good news and as an outworking of the presence of the Spirit

128 Charles Gusmer, *The Ministry of Healing in the Church of England: An Ecumenical-liturgical Study,* Mayhew McCrimmon, 1974, p. 126.

in the life of the Church.'[129] The opening collect in *A Celebration of Wholeness and Healing* underlines the focus on salvation and the church:

Anoint your Church with the same Holy Spirit,
that we who share in his suffering and victory
may bear witness to the gospel of salvation.

There is much in the CW *Wholeness and Healing* material that could still be explored in the local church:

- Finding ways of embedding healing both within the normal life of the church and within the life of the local community. As the CW *Introduction* says: 'Prayer for healing needs to take seriously the way in which individual sickness and vulnerability are often the result of injustice and social oppression'. This might involve the church in being vulnerable and recognizing its own need of healing. That might be a prerequisite for the healing of the society and culture in which the church is placed.

  This personal ministry may be offered at one of the following points:
  – as part of the Prayers of Intercession ...
  – at the time of the giving of communion ...
  – at the end of the service.[130]

- One way of embedding healing in the 'normal' life of the church is to offer the laying on of hands (and/or anointing) every week. CWPS page 48 suggests three places where this might happen in the main service. We need to move away from treating healing as an optional extra for a small group of enthusiasts at a time when most of the church is not present. Prayer ministers should be carefully chosen and trained.
- If healing is a normal part of church life, it should also be a normal part of teaching, formation and worship, as well as the pastoral ministry of the church, following the pattern of James 5.

129 In parallel with the Liturgical Commission's work, the House of Bishops commissioned a report, *A Time to Heal*, GS 1378, CHP, 2000.
130 CWPS, p. 48.

The strong background of baptismal theology, scriptural allusions and texts in these CW services should also lead the local church to explore both mission and ministry. So, if all are baptized and therefore responsible for ministering to one another, the whole congregation should be taught

> Theologians and therapists alike have explored the idea that somebody who has suffered, or is still suffering, can minister healing to others.[131]

about praying for one another, laying on hands if appropriate. This can be done in the context of families or groups praying for one another at home, or in church where anyone wanting prayer is invited to sit or kneel just where they are while those around pray for them. If all sit they can take turns – surely everyone in the church is in need of *some* healing.

Looking ahead

The vibrant church of the future will not only be equipping all the baptized for this ministry, but finding ways of engaging with the local community. For instance, using the main *Celebration of Wholeness and Healing* service from time to time in the local church, rather than reserving it for 'big' occasions (as the notes suggest) would create an opportunity, with suitable preparation through the local and social media, backed with specific invitations, to involve the local community, over time, in an exploration of the relationship between such things as reconciliation, vulnerability and wholeness. What about a public dialogue with some local figure? The 'Sending Out' dialogue at the end of the Celebration service captures some of this result of being made whole:

> God who said: Let light shine out of darkness
> **has caused his light to shine within us ...**
> We have this treasure in earthen vessels
> **to show that the power belongs to God.**

---

131 See, for example, Henri Nouwen, *The Wounded Healer*, Doubleday, 1979.

Why are people not healed today?

- Because we live in a fallen world.
- Because no one speaks to Jesus about them (Luke 4.38).
- Because they have no friends who will bring them to Jesus (Luke 4.40).
- Because we have a wrong attitude to sickness.
- Because we have a wrong attitude to the medical profession (cf 2 Chron. 16.12).
- Because we do not ask (James 5).
- Because there is no faith or expectation that Jesus will heal (Matt. 17.14–21).
- Because of sin, though in the story of the man born blind (John 9.1–12) Jesus makes it clear that sickness or disability is not necessarily caused by sin.
- Because we are not willing to accept the whole package on offer, healing in mind and body, peace with God and others.

TO THINK ABOUT

- What healing have I experienced from God?
- What wounds do I bear that may not be healed?
- How am I seeking to be made 'whole' today?
- To whom can I admit my need to be healed?
- Who can minister that to me, on God's behalf?

TO DISCUSS

- To what extent is your congregation engaged in a ministry of healing?
- Suggest one or two ways in which the church could move forward in this.

C7

SILENCE

Experiences of silence, and the value attached to them, vary from person to person, according to both the personality and the background of each. Here is a story from John Leach:

> Next door to the office where I work is the Lincoln School of Theology. Every day from 12 noon until 12.15 the staff and students join in prayer in the Bishop's Chapel, guided by the striking of the Cathedral clock, in whose shadow it lies. After brief initial biddings, we spend 15 minutes in silence. Then the clock strikes quarter past and we all go back to work.
>
> The first time I was invited to join in this prayer time the unreconstructed evangelical in me reacted by thinking that this was not a 'proper' time of prayer, since no one actually said anything. But I have since come to value it as a cool, calm oasis in the middle of a busy working day, and it has often been a time of close communion with God.

The value of silence

Silence is of itself counter-cultural in a noisy world. In fact, we seem to be so uncomfortable with silence that we constantly try to fill it at home, in the car, in shops, and in church.

In a frantic world silence is a rare commodity, and yet TV programmes such as *The Monastery*, in which a group of people who are 'not religious' live for a period within the cloisters of a monastic community, often with life-changing results, have whetted our appetites for a chance to step off the treadmill and reconnect with something deeper and more still. Of course dabbling in various forms of meditation has been fashionable among a minority since the hippy years of the 1960s and 70s, but for many people a more mature yearning for something other than noise and hurry appears to be on the increase.

Richard Foster's classic *Celebration of Discipline* has become a guidebook for several generations of those wishing to explore the spiritual disciplines, and his chapters on solitude and meditation set out a vision of a less hurried, less harassed lifestyle. Martin Saunders' reworking of this subject, aimed more specifically at today's youth, uses the same disciplines and continues to extol their virtues. He defines the discipline of solitude as 'the practice of silence and listening for the voice of God in that silence ... [it] is the act of taking ourselves out of the busyness of everyday life, of seeking God in the silence of retreat' (p. 129).[132]

For some, spending an extended time in silence, without moving, will be excruciatingly difficult – but for them silence becomes refreshing if accompanied by an activity such as walking, art or craft.

Silence in worship

So if silence is such a potentially valuable commodity in today's world, we ought to find it holding a central place in Christian worship, where and when we specifically take time out to encounter God. But in churches both liturgical and non-liturgical this is seldom the case. In some places there will be half an hour or more of non-stop singing, followed by up to an hour of listening. In others hymns and other ingredients will follow hot-foot after one another, while in Anglican churches the diet might consist of the stream of words as the BCP texts are read, or the pick'n'mix concoctions of *Common Worship*. So where can we be silent?

The main CW services do tell us in rubrics that silence is encouraged in a couple of places during the services, although

---

132 Richard Foster, *Celebration of Discipline,* Hodder & Stoughton, 1980; Martin Saunders, *The Beautiful Disciplines,* Monarch, 2011.

the question of how or even whether those silences are used is one to which we must return. But it is worth noting that in the Holy Communion service silence is recommended before the collect of the day and before the post-Communion prayer (unless the opening Form of Preparation is used, in which case there is a space for silence for reflection between the Beatitudes and the confession). Morning and Evening Prayer suggest silence after the opening prayers ('The night has passed ...' and 'That this evening may be holy ...') after each of the Bible readings, and possibly as part of the intercessions. Night Prayer, as one might expect, has a little more silence, but not that much; at the start and before the confession to recollect the day past, and during the intercessions again, although there is the custom that the service concludes with the people leaving in silence.

The Service of the Word fares better, and the introductory notes ask us to consider, when planning the service, whether there is enough silence, and suggest that it 'may be kept at different points of the service. It may be particularly appropriate at the beginning of the service, after the readings and the sermon, and during the prayers.'[133]

Even if worship leaders do keep these periods of silence (though experience suggests that few do), there are often problems with the ways they are used. They are often severely truncated, so that no time is allowed for us to settle into the quiet, and there is seldom any help given as to why we are keeping this silence and what we are meant to be doing with it. Alternatively we are given so much instruction that the silence is covered with introduction, which often lasts far longer than the silence itself. So we ask three simple questions:

• Within the liturgy of *Common Worship*, when might we appropriately use silence?
• Why might we use it?
• And how might we use it?

---

133 CW Service of the Word, note 4, p. 26.

What does silence do? Silences within liturgy (and I am not primarily talking here about extended periods of silence which dominate a gathering, or even more substantial retreats) function like commas, to give us a pause, to allow us to stop, settle down and go more deeply into what is happening and what God might be saying to us through it. One of the reasons for not reading a sermon from a full script is that it can then be a bit too slick, and comes at the congregation relentlessly without a break. Normal speech would always contain a few pauses, 'um's and 'er's, which function to break up the flow of words and allow them some breathing space. Silence in the liturgy functions in the same way: it allows us to stop and think, or even to stop and feel.

Silence in the Eucharist

Different points in the service will suggest different kinds of silence.

If we begin **before the service** starts, we immediately hit a tension. Some believe that reverent silence is the only appropriate way to approach worship, while others enjoy the buzz and conversation of the 'family' gathering together, and make the point that any family which gathered in silence would most likely be going to a funeral, not a celebration. There is no easy answer here, but many churches negotiate this dilemma by allowing the gathering buzz, then using the notices for the week before the service proper begins, and asking for a few minutes silence before the ministers enter and worship begins. This works well once it is established that latecomers who are coming into the silence do so sensitively, and do not attempt to restart the buzz, but generally congregations get this and value it.

If the service does not begin in this way, it might be appropriate **after the greeting** or opening hymn to allow some space for people to focus on where they are and what they are doing, before summing up this silence in the Collect for Purity.

Before **confession** we might want to dwell on the day or week past and allow the Spirit to bring to our minds items which might particularly need attention (note that this is different from trying to dredge up everything nasty we have done, said or thought).

The silence **before the collect** is introduced in many churches with an introductory sentence which picks up both the theme of the collect and the issue to be addressed in preaching later. An appropriate sentence for Trinity Sunday might be something like, 'Let us pray that we may know God as Father, Son and Holy Spirit ...' which gives people a way to use the silence, picks up the theme and the collect, but doesn't merely duplicate what the collect is going to say in a moment. Silence is then kept, and the collect is said by the president.

Readings are obvious places for silence, but as well as allowing space for reflection after we have heard them, how about before, as we take time to invite God to speak to us through what we are about to receive? Or how about saving 'This is the word of the Lord ...' until after people have had a chance to reflect on it? If we use a psalm the monastic tradition of keeping a long pause at the half-way point of each verse might be used, although experience shows that this works better in smaller groups praying the offices than in greater congregations. The more people there are, the greater the possibility of a machine-gun start each time.

It is sometimes argued that **preaching** ought to call forth some kind of a response, and the use of silence at the end of an address can provide opportunity for this to happen in a variety of ways. A simple meditation may be led by the preacher, which allows people to personalize what they have heard and think about what this actually means to them, where they are in this story, what the Spirit might be calling them to do as a response, and so on. Or a simple question may prompt some silent meditation: 'What is the one thing which you feel most spoke to you out of what you have heard, read and preached this morning?'[134]

> As people arrive to worship in the chapel at Taizé they are welcomed by smiling young people holding large signs saying 'Silence' in a variety of languages.

---

134 John Leach, *Responding to Preaching*, GBW 139, 1997.

LIntercessions can use silence in a variety of ways, and we are probably most familiar with its use here. Occasionally it might be appropriate to cut spoken words down to a minimum, and simply keep an extended period of silence: this works well as long as you let people know that this is what is intended, so that they don't think that the service leader has dropped off. Silence accompanied by some kind of action can be powerful too. Candles may be lit, or some other active prayer may be used.

We are used to keeping silence on Remembrance Sunday as a mark of respect for the fallen, but this might also be used for intercession on the occasion of a major disaster for which we are praying. In church two miles from Hillsborough stadium the day after that fateful day in April 1989, nobody knew quite how to pray, and silence was the most appropriate and honest response. There will be other occasions like that.

The Peace is a part of the service rather like Marmite: you either love it or hate it. So how about ringing the changes and pausing **before the Eucharistic Prayer** with a period of silence, ending with the words 'The Lord is here'?

Silence **during the Eucharistic Prayers** is not encouraged, but one possible way to create some space might be to use the section occupied by the proper preface 'And now we give you thanks ...' to encourage the congregation to use silence to think about what they find themselves most thankful for today. Again, the silence can be ended with the liturgical words, 'Therefore with angels and archangels ...' and on into the *Sanctus*. We just need to be careful not to break the momentum of the prayer with too long a gap at this point. A substantial silence **at the end of the prayer** is good not least for the president to get his or her breath back, but also for the whole congregation to stop and appreciate the presence of God. The longer I leave this silence, the deeper it seems to get. Communion might be received in silence for a change, rather than being accompanied by music and/or singing: this would be appropriate during more austere and penitent periods of the year. And as the rubrics suggest, to pause at the end of the distribution before rushing onwards to the end can be a helpful thing.

This is merely a list of suggestions, but as a general guide anything which might slow down the headlong rush of the liturgy and provide some airholes and breathing space is to be welcomed, and any point in the service where there is deeper connection with the text, with God or with his word is fair game for us to stop and pause.

Leading silence

Finally, a few words about how we might lead silence. A few years ago, a rubric in an order of service from Coventry Cathedral stated that at a certain point there will be 'a profound silence'. How do you make a silence a profound one? We all know it when we experience it, and worship leaders need to know how to lead silence helpfully. They need, I believe, to do three things: introduce it, time it, and close it appropriately. If we are going to use a period of silence, people need to be helped into it. They need to know that it is deliberate, not someone forgetting their lines, they need an approximate guide to how long it might be for, so that they don't think the leader has forgotten them, and they need some general clue as to what they might usefully do with it. So simply to stop after a Bible reading does none of these three, whereas to say something like, 'We'll now keep a minute or two's silence to think about what struck us from that reading' does all three. Silent intercession might be introduced with 'We're going to keep an extended time of quiet while we pray for the victims of that earthquake, and those who are seeking to help them. You might like to pray for someone there just like you: what would you be feeling, wanting, hoping …'

Paradoxically, silence is sometimes best if it is not silent. Particularly if movement is involved ('If you would like to, come and light a candle and pray for someone you know who is ill …') it can actually feel more silent if some quiet ambient music is playing at a low volume, to cover the sound of shuffling and footsteps.

Children and silence do not always go well together, but they too can feel its value, so it is helpful if a church culture is created where parents understand that while at times it is fine for their kids to run around and chatter, there are other times when they need to be helped by their carers to stop and focus on God. With their low concentration spans it might not be wise to use extended periods of silence when children are present at all-age worship, but with help they ought to be able to manage a few moments.

Another thing to remember is that your watch goes twice as fast when you are facing west as when you're facing east. In other words, for nervous worship leaders a one-minute silence can feel like 100 years, while for the congregation it can seem you have rounded it off before you have even started. So hold your nerve, and use your watch to time what you have decided is an appropriate period of silence. Leaders invariably want to move on well before the people are ready to.

Rounding off silence needs to give a clear indication that we are moving on. An appropriate line from the liturgy is good: 'Lord, in your mercy ...', 'Merciful Father ...', or maybe an extempore prayer to sum up what we have hopefully been doing: 'Thank you Lord for your word: may you continue to speak to us as we move on'. Another possibility is to have the musicians play the introduction to the next hymn.

In a world increasingly hungry for peace and quiet, and in buildings which in popular opinion are made for it, we need to take on a few simple attitudes and practices which will help provide silences, and make them as 'profound' as we can.

TO THINK ABOUT

- When has your own experience of silence been positive? Or negative?

TO DISCUSS

- How does 'stillness' differ from 'silence'?
- Share two or three suggestions from this chapter which might be worth trying.

C8

MUSICAL

Music is an important part of human culture. Most of us hear music on a daily basis, even if we ourselves do not sing.

It has been said that worship without music does not easily soar. So while there will undoubtedly always be services with no singing or instrumental music, most congregations (whatever their resources) will want to draw in some way on the rich potential which music offers – in fact, congregational song has come to play an increasingly dominant part in the worship of some churches in recent decades.

How does music work?

Looking at ways in which music functions as we worship can inspire fresh exploration; it can help musicians and other leaders (lay or ordained) to be 'reflective practitioners', making discerning choices:

- Singing helps to form community, enabling a corporate response and a shared repertoire of praise and prayer. For members of the body of Christ, young and old, music provides a way of using a variety of gifts and encourages the offering of service. It can also draw in those exploring faith. Music plays a vital part in mission: attracting, playing a role in proclamation, and energizing those sent out in the power of the Spirit to love and serve the Lord. This can include instrumental music, from a thrilling organ voluntary to the improvizations of a jazz band.[135]

---

135 John Leach, *Thirty Ways to Use Music in Worship*, GBW 209, 2011.

- Music enables God's people to fulfil the biblical injunction to 'sing a new song to the Lord' and allows the word of Christ to 'dwell in us richly' as we sing 'psalms, hymns and spiritual songs' to God and to one another. It helps us to bring our whole selves into our worship: body, mind and emotions, our full humanity. What opportunities and resources are there for singing biblical texts or words clearly inspired by scripture?[136]

- Music, both vocal and instrumental, facilitates the joyful expression of praise, the sighs of penitence and longing, and the tears of lament. It can evoke atmosphere and heighten drama. As the bearer of text it illuminates meaning, makes it more memorable, and enables it to be shared and savoured by performers and listeners; it can 'stretch' words, allowing for reflection and engagement. Sung worship helps to form theological understanding through its words and moods, and shapes habits of praise and prayer. We often carry a song or part of a hymn with us on leaving church, probably remembering it better than the sermon![137] (See also D1 To Become More Like Jesus.)

  'Music has the uncanny ability to burrow its way into our spiritual bones.' *John Witvliet*

- Music and silence help articulate the structure and dynamics of the liturgy and the seasons of the Church Year: the words and music we sing at Christmas, for example, will be significantly different from those associated with Good Friday, in both content and mood, and music intended for Advent or Lent is unlikely to be helpful in the Easter season. Music heard at specific times each year builds up powerful associations,

---

136 Anne Harrison, *Recovering the Lord's Song: Getting Sung Scripture Back into Worship*, GBW 198, 2009.

137 Rosalind Brown, *How Hymns Shape our Lives*, Grove Books, Spirituality 78, 2001.

and this has perhaps been undervalued in recent evangelical worship. Can we find opportunities for short repeated chants, perhaps combined with spoken seasonal text, to provide a reflective space in worship, to enable intercession, or to lift the spirits?[138]

- Music also enables us to prepare for and join in the worship of heaven – in his vision recounted in Revelation, John heard myriads of angels singing and saw a great multitude from every nation, tribe, people and language crying out, 'Salvation belongs to our God, who sits on the throne, and to the Lamb'.
- Singing can function as an expression of identity and enables us to express solidarity with the worldwide Church and the communion of saints, as we incorporate hymns and songs from different times and places into our worship. We would love to see those who plan music for worship reflecting on the words of Jesus, found in Matthew 13, when he said teachers who become disciples in the kingdom of heaven could be like 'the owner of a house who brings out of his storeroom new treasures as well as old'.[139] (See also A1 Relational.)

TO DISCUSS

- How might we encourage singers and instrumentalists from our congregation or local community to offer their gifts in worship?
- Are we exploring a range of new sung material alongside our familiar repertoire?
- Do we take advantage of the role of sung worship in Christian learning and development?
- Might we find a way to assess the theological content as well as 'singability' of new hymns and songs?

---

138 Anne Harrison, *Sing it Again: The Place of Short Songs in Worship*, GBW 176, 2003.

139 Mark Earey, *How to Choose Songs and Hymns for Worship*, GBW 201, 2009.

- Are there ways of enhancing seasonal worship, for example with short repeated chants, perhaps combined with spoken seasonal text, to provide a reflective space in worship, to enable intercession, or to provide a punctuation of praise in our worship?
- How can we help those who choose what we sing to draw on words and music from various eras and parts of the world?

Precisely because music is such a powerful element in worship, and people often feel a strong emotional attachment to particular styles and repertoire, what is played and sung can become a focus of division within a congregation, or between musicians and other leaders of worship. Building up trust and mutual respect is crucial. How can we provide opportunities for constructive dialogue and regular review among those who plan and lead music?

What is on the menu?

Common Worship in all its variety provides ample scope for good stewardship of the precious tradition of inherited musical forms and for the development and nurturing of new ones. The particular music we cherish will depend largely on our own background, cultural and spiritual. In incorporating both old and new musical styles and forms into our worship, the human and technical resources we have available will play a major part. Let's consider some of the types of Christian music used over the centuries:

Seen in a supermarket: 'Why not try something you can't pronounce?'

Plainsong is probably the most ancient style of singing still in use in some contexts today, particularly in religious communities. It consists of a single line of vocal music (though it is sometimes accompanied) and does not usually have a regular metre or pattern of stresses, so it is a versatile vehicle for carrying many kinds of text. Recordings of Gregorian chant in Latin have proved hugely popular in recent years, perhaps reflecting a longing for mystery and transcendence. Playing a track to accompany visual images on a screen can be very atmospheric, perhaps leading into confession or intercession.

> The tune normally used for 'Come, Holy Ghost, our souls inspire' (often sung at ordinations) is a plainsong hymn.

Simple chant, singing most syllables of a verse on a single 'reciting note' (in unison or harmony) along with one or more other notes afterwards, can be an effective way for a group worshipping regularly to sing biblical texts; underlining or italics indicate when to move to the next note. Over the past 50 years or so, increasing numbers of churches have used responsorial psalms in which one or more voices chant the verses, interspersed with congregational refrains which are more rhythmic and conventionally melodic. These may help to reintroduce psalm-singing where it has dropped out of the repertoire, especially if one or two singers can act as cantors.

Some of these psalm settings come from Roman Catholic sources – James MacMillan is a well-respected Scottish composer who takes this genre seriously in his own parish context.

Anglican chant, like plainsong and simple chant, enables biblical poetry (*psalms and canticles*) with lines of varying lengths to be sung to a repeated tune, usually in four-part harmony, accompanied by an organ. A system of lines and dots known as 'pointing' is provided with the verses so that singers and accompanists know how to fit the words to the music. Some congregations enjoy

> Listen to the psalms during *Choral Evensong* on BBC Radio 3 for a good demonstration of Anglican chant.

this style of chanting once they have had some practice, but on the whole it is more effective when left to trained choirs. (See B3 Using the Psalms.)

Choral liturgical settings. Many composers have set texts from the BCP and CW, whether for Holy Communion or services of Morning and Evening Prayer, often for cathedral, college or

Sometimes appropriate hymns or songs can be substituted for exact settings of liturgical texts. At the reburial of King Richard III in Leicester Cathedral in 2015 the service included a metrical paraphrase of the Song of Zechariah (*Benedictus*) sung by choir and congregation to the hymn tune Corvedale.

parish choirs though also, less frequently, as congregational settings. The usual eucharistic settings include the *Kyrie* (Lord, have mercy), the *Gloria* (Glory to God in the highest), the *Sanctus* (Holy, holy) and the *Agnus Dei* (Lamb of God); sometimes the Creed is also set to music. Several recent hymn books include simple settings of these texts, or metrical paraphrases, for congregations.[140]

CW Order One provides for a sung or spoken Gospel Alleluia, choral or congregational, to 'herald the reading'. At Matins and Evensong choirs often sing responses and canticles (such as the *Magnificat*, the Song of Mary, and *Nunc Dimittis*, the Song of Simeon) on behalf of the congregation, who either join in or participate by listening and making the words of the sung prayer their own internally.

Anthems sung by choirs and small vocal ensembles, with or without instrumental accompaniment, who can enrich the people's worship and make their own offering to God by performing musical compositions with words appropriate to the occasion and the stage in the journey through worship. These help to celebrate creativity and imagination, a vital aspect of humankind made in the image of God the Creator. Some anthems or vocal solos are particularly suitable for weddings or funerals; others may be sung at the start of a service, during the distribution of communion, or as a reflection before or after a sermon or prayers. Texts include Bible verses, hymns (such as John Rutter's 'For the beauty of

Anthems don't need to be classical: gospel choirs can give a fresh and more contemporary flavour.

---

140 See *Ancient and Modern: Hymns and Songs for Refreshing Worship*, Canterbury Press, 2013.

the earth') and prayers. Some anthems are parts of longer works such as Handel's *Messiah*.

Hymns. The main musical role in a service for most congregations tends to be singing hymns, introduced into Church of England worship from the late eighteenth century, at first without official approval (though metrical psalms have been permitted since the Reformation). The texts normally have several verses, each using the same poetic metre and rhyme scheme and sung to the same tune (which may also suit other hymns in that metre). Words and music are usually written by different people. Most traditional hymn tunes are composed in four-part harmony and sung either unaccompanied or with organ or piano accompaniment, although there are plenty of stirring 'unison' tunes, where all voices sing the melody. Inviting women to sing one of the verses and men to sing another can help sustain interest and drama. Musicians such as Ralph Vaughan Williams and, more recently, John Bell of the Iona Community have encouraged the use of folk melodies in hymn-singing (such as the English tune 'Kingsfold' for 'I heard the voice of Jesus say' and the Scottish 'Ye banks and braes' for 'We cannot measure how you heal'). These work well where there is no accompaniment available.

> Introducing a new hymn or song by having it sung by a soloist or group the week before inviting the congregation to sing it may sometimes help.

New hymn texts, using contemporary language and often exploring a wider range of themes than in traditional hymnody, can most easily be introduced when sung to well-known melodies; however, learning the occasional new tune helps to keep the repertoire fresh. Words by writers such as Timothy Dudley-Smith (b. 1926) and Martin Leckebusch (b. 1962) provide a rich resource to explore and deserve musical settings suitable for congregations led by a praise band as well as those singing with an organ or piano.[141] Samuel Thompson (b. 1987) is one musician working in this field.

---

141 See, for example, the Jubilate website (www.jubilate.co.uk).

Settings of old hymn texts to music in more contemporary styles, suitable for music groups, are currently popular; examples include Vikki Cook's 'Before the throne of God above'. Often a refrain is added to the original verses, as in the new version of 'What a friend we have in Jesus' by Pete James. Keith Getty and Stuart Townend have championed the writing of 'modern hymns', with music and words written as a unit, taking a relatively casual approach to rhyme and using a musical style more often associated with 'worship songs' – their best-known collaboration is 'In Christ alone'. They seek theological depth and integrity in their texts, and have attempted to broaden the subject matter of contemporary Christian music.

Hymns on important topics like justice and peace, healing or environmental concern, are easier to find in recently written material.

Worship songs and choruses. The distinction between hymns and songs has become more difficult to make, with hymns increasingly sung by praise bands and some Christian songwriters producing substantial texts with multiple verses. Most often the words and music of a 'chorus' (originally referring to the refrain of a hymn or song) are by the same person, frequently a guitarist, meaning that the musical focus may be harmonic and rhythmic rather than melodic. While the music can be written down for use by others, what is on the page needs to be interpreted more freely than in hymns or choral music, and worship groups often learn songs from recordings. Several songs may be sung in succession as a 'set', and space allowed for improvization or singing in the Spirit. Sometimes songs heard on recordings or at festivals and conferences work well for a solo vocalist with a really good band but not so well for congregations – worship leaders choosing or teaching new songs need

Musical styles include folk, rock (ideally with drums, electric guitar and keyboard) and gospel (usually with a soloist and choir). Amplification and balance normally require someone operating a sound-desk.

to think whether the key, melody and rhythm (and volume!) will encourage everyone to join in.[142]

Songs from the world Church, using music sung by Christians in other parts of the globe, is a concrete expression of our belief in 'the holy catholic Church'. We can sing in solidarity with those who suffer in specific places, and to undergird our prayers for brothers and sisters around the world. Short songs from Africa (such as 'Siyahamba' – 'We are marching in the light of God') or elsewhere appeal to all ages without being trite.[143]

Short chants, simple musical units, repeated a number of times, can enrich worship in various ways. If sung continuously, perhaps during a time of reflection, symbolic action or contemplative prayer, they are often called 'chants'. Among the best-known music in this form is the repertoire developed by the ecumenical Taizé Community in France (e.g. Jacques Berthier's 'Eat this bread', often sung during the distribution of bread and wine), but there are also examples from the Iona Community and among the songs and choral music written by Margaret Rizza. Might your musicians find or arrange a training event where they can learn more about these styles?

> Short songs taught by rote are particularly useful in all-age worship and other contexts where literacy levels vary or different languages are spoken.

Sung prayer responses, interspersing spoken petitions with a musical response in prayers of thanksgiving or intercession, can engage the emotions as well as the mind, fostering the heart-felt participation of all in the prayer. One example is John Bell's 'Through our lives and by our prayers, your kingdom come'. Where the technology is available to project images, the combination of spoken and sung prayer with appropriate visual

---

142 Nick Drake, *A Deeper Note: The 'Informal' Theology of Sung Worship,* GBW 218, 2014.

143 The Iona Community's Wild Goose Publications are one useful source.

material can be very powerful. Can you encourage those who lead intercessions to liaise with musicians over an occasional sung response? It is possible to use different words, set to the same tune, in different parts of the service.

Using a cantor, a solo singer who can help to lead the congregation in various ways, from teaching a new song, or singing verses in a psalm or song between refrains sung by all, to providing an extra melodic line above Taizé chants to enrich the musical and verbal material. At a wedding, funeral or baptism with non-churchgoers present, a cantor can transform the musical possibilities. Do you have a confident singer who is also spiritually sensitive who might take on this role?

Instrumental music. There are occasions when a piece of music without words (live or recorded) can provide valuable reflective space or allow for movement, perhaps to different prayer stations. Creative ways of combining speech with instrumental music can engage interest: a psalm might be read while an ensemble plays a piece with appropriate atmosphere, for example, or with a carefully selected piece of recorded music in the background.

If our Christian faith is shaped at least in part by what we sing, it is important that our sung worship should be theologically rich and explicitly trinitarian. This has implications for songwriters and all those who choose hymns, songs and anthems week by week.

> We train our worship leaders in being Spirit-sensitive, in the art of the sound system, in how to link songs well, in the use of PowerPoint, and in personal intimacy with God. Why don't we also teach a robust Trinitarian theology as well as a theology of worship as an essential component of their craft?[144]

---

144 Robin Parry, *Worshipping Trinity: Coming Back to the Heart of Worship*, Paternoster, 2005.

Looking forward

It is exciting to see so much new music being produced by contemporary songwriters (and copyright licences from CCL and Calamus have made its use much simpler). However, for theological depth, breadth of style and our sense of being part of a historic community of faith, we have a responsibility to draw on the best of what has been valued by earlier generations, as well as developing the tradition for those who will follow us. We worship a God who created an extraordinarily diverse world for human beings, animals, birds and fish to live in – perhaps an inspiration for our own creativity?

Music done badly can wreck any act of worship, but trying something new inevitably carries an element of risk. Musicians need to be given permission to experiment, but it is worth remembering that it may require something simple done imaginatively and well for the music – and with it the worship – to take flight.

> Blessed are you, Lord God,
> our light and our salvation;
> to you be glory and praise for ever.
>
> From the beginning you have created all things
> and all your works echo the silent music of your praise ...
>
> You give us breath and speech, that with angels and archangels
> and all the powers of heaven
> we may find a voice to sing your praise.[145]

---

145 CW Order One, Eucharistic Prayer G.

'Worship should be ...
or should involve ...'

D:
SENDING

D1

TO BECOME MORE LIKE JESUS

While Christian worship is primarily something offered by human beings to God, there can be significant spin-offs for the lives of the worshippers and the lives of those around them. 'Good' worship should transform lives and transform society, changing character and challenging culture. (See D4 Prophetic.)

Christians should be different from the rest of fallen humanity – not only by the name they claim, their T-shirts, jewellery, or bumper stickers, but in the way they live. At the end of an act of worship the worshippers should not see themselves as dispersing to carry on as before. Rather, in worship people should recognize they are transformed by their encounter with the living God and sent out in turn to transform the world.

> Not everyone who says to me, 'Lord, Lord', will enter the kingdom of heaven, but only one who does the will of my Father in heaven. (Matt. 7.21)

Those who truly acknowledge Jesus Christ as their King will do the King's will and be part of his kingdom on earth, as well as looking towards his heavenly kingdom. What God has done for us in Christ not only reverses Adam's fall, replacing disobedience with obedience, but ultimately lifts us higher. As we move more deeply into communion with Christ, we become more like Christ.

Jesus himself speaks not of his disciples becoming like him, but of mutual indwelling, telling them that he and the Father and the Spirit will live in them, and that they will live in him (John 14.17, 20, 23). He encourages them to remain in him, so that they will bear fruit (John 15.4–6). The theme is briefly echoed in his subsequent prayer to the Father (John 17.21–23).

L John rehearses the same idea of indwelling in his first letter, linking it with obedience, and living like Jesus (1 John 2.6, 24–27; 3.24, 4.15–17).

Paul, however, uses the metaphor of clothing, when he writes to the church in Galatia: 'As many of you as were baptized into Christ have clothed yourselves with Christ' (Gal. 3.27).

To the Corinthians Paul writes with the stronger image of transformation – the Greek word that he uses is the origin of our English 'metamorphosis' used to describe a caterpillar changing into a butterfly: 'We all, who with unveiled faces contemplate the Lord's glory, are being transformed into his image with ever-increasing glory, which comes from the Lord, who is the Spirit' (2 Cor. 3.18).

A further dimension to our transformation is our growing unity with one another – as sheep in a flock, stones in a building, a family, members of the body of Christ.

So we may consider how our worship contributes to this indwelling, this clothing, this metamorphosis, this unification. The German philosopher, Feuerbach, is often quoted as saying that man is what he eats. We are shaped by the words and experiences that come our way during our lives. Rich, well-crafted worship should shape those who engage with it.

Transformation through words of scripture

We need not dwell long on this here, as it is covered elsewhere. We want to underline the importance of scripture as a key component of our worship. The reading of the Bible should not be neglected in the church services of the third millennium. In the Bible we hear about the greatness, love and power of God. We discover what God has done for his people over the millennia, and we are challenged to respond in praise, confession, thanksgiving and action. We are reminded of who God is, who we are, and who we should be, setting us on the track for transformation. (See B2 Biblical.)

We should read all of the Bible, Old Testament and New, narrative and prophecy and letters and legal material, the easy parts and the difficult parts. They are all to be read, for 'all scripture is inspired by God and is useful for teaching, for reproof, for correction, and for training in righteousness, so that everyone who belongs to God may be proficient, equipped for every good work' (2 Tim. 3.16, 17).

It is natural to shy away from the parts of God's word which are hard to understand, or which portray God in a way which conflicts with our own image of the divine. For example, one might be tempted to avoid texts touching on:

- Zionism;
- homosexuality;
- warfare;
- the wrath of God;
- the end times.

It is, however, possible to look at such passages in their context, and explore how conflicting contemporary positions can be justified in scripture.

The age-old tradition of including at least two readings and a psalm in an act of worship has much to commend it. Lectionaries make sure that we encounter the full breadth of God's word, but should be seen as aids to greater understanding rather than legalistic straitjackets, and may be set aside if circumstances require. (See B2 Biblical, box on the Lectionary.) Within the *Common Worship* provision there is permission to go 'off piste' at certain times of year. This can be used to good advantage, whether to address particular needs in the local church, or to explore a biblical book or a theme in depth. By exercising their pastoral vision ministers can provide the nourishment for people to grow more like Jesus.

Transformation through words of worship

The words that we use in our prayers and in our songs, many of which are repeated month by month, become part of our thinking, and influence who we are and how we act. Words of praise serve a transformatory function, in that we are reminded of the greatness of God compared with the relative insignificance of our own lives; reminded that the universe does not revolve around us.

Nevertheless, in our worship we also find many phrases pointing to the changes that should be happening in our lives, our progression towards the second Adam seen in Christ.

The table below reviews some varied examples.

'Cleanse the thoughts of our hearts by the inspiration of your Holy Spirit' (Prayer of Preparation, CW p. 168)	We are aware of our impurity: we ask to be made pure.
'Forgive what we have been, help us to amend what we are, and direct what we shall be; that we may do justly, love mercy, and walk humbly with you, our God.' (Prayer of Penitence, CW p. 169)	Note the trajectory from past to future, and the two emphases of who we are and how we live. The text draws on Micah 6.8.
'... form us into the likeness of Christ and make us a perfect offering in your sight.' (Eucharistic Prayer F, CW p. 199)	An explicit prayer for our transformation, not for our own benefit but to be an offering to God.

'Though we are many, we are one body, because we all share in one bread.' (Breaking of the Bread, CW p. 179)	Not a prayer, but an outright declaration of our unity.
'Lord, I am not worthy to receive you, but only say the word, and I shall be healed.' (Giving of Communion, CW p. 180)	A transformation from past unworthiness to future wholeness, not in our own strength but through the grace of God. The text draws on the story of the centurion in Matthew 8.
'...that he may live in us and we in him.' (Prayer before the distribution, CW p. 181)	This picks up the theme of mutual indwelling from Jesus' words at the Last Supper, as we prepare to receive 'the precious body and blood' into our own bodies.
'Send us out in the power of your Spirit to live and work to your praise and glory.' (Prayers after Communion, CW p. 182)	We are sent out not just to complete a programme of action, but to live in a new way.

Words of transformation found in traditional hymns

'O let me see thy footmarks, and in them plant mine own ...' ('O Jesus I have promised', John Bode)	The singer commits not only to following, but to placing their feet precisely in the footprints of their master.

'Take my will and make it thine, it shall be no longer mine. Take my heart, it is thine own, it shall be thy royal throne.' ('Take my life and let it be', Frances Havergal)	This hymn is a commitment to complete identification with Christ – hands, feet, lips, heart and will.
'Be thou my wisdom, be thou my true word, be thou ever with me, and I with thee Lord; be thou my great Father, and I thy true son; be thou in me dwelling, and I with thee one.' ('Be thou my vision', Eleanor Hull)	Not only side-by-side, not only a parent–child relationship, but mutual indwelling.
'Called out from every nation, yet one o'er all the earth; her charter of salvation, one Lord, one faith, one birth; one holy Name she blesses, partakes one holy food, and to one hope she presses, with every grace endued.' ('The Church's one foundation', Samuel Stone)	The first verse of this hymn speaks of the Church as the bride of Christ; this second verse speaks of the unity of Christians within the Church.
'In Christ now meet both East and West, in him meet South and North, all Christly souls are one in him, throughout the whole wide earth.' ('In Christ there is no East or West', John Oxenham)	This hymn speaks of the unity of all Christians, regardless of geography or race.

Words of transformation in modern worship songs

These are drawn from the 'UK churches' chart published by Christian Copyright Licensing International.[146]

'From life's first cry to final breath, Jesus commands my destiny ... Till He returns or calls me home – Here in the pow'r of Christ I'll stand.' ('In Christ alone', Keith Getty and Stuart Townend)	The singer looks at the life, death and resurrection of Jesus Christ, and proclaims total commitment to and dependence on him.
'And I will trust in you alone.' ('The Lord's my shepherd', Stuart Townend)	The song is a metrical version of Psalm 23, which has an implicit message of trust in God; but Townend adds this explicit expression of trust, sung twice in each refrain, so that the song becomes a powerful forward-looking commitment, as the singer abandons other sources of security. The haunting descant 'I will trust, I will trust in you' adds to the effect.

---

146 See uk.ccli.com/.

'Your majesty, I can but bow, I lay my all before you now. In royal robes I don't deserve I live to serve your majesty.' ('King of kings', Jarrod Cooper)	Again, complete dedication to service; the 'robes I don't deserve' remind us of the robing of the prodigal son, and Paul's clothing metaphor in Galatians – but the adjective 'royal' invites us to identify with our king, given that we have been adopted into the divine royal family.
'I will offer up my life in spirit and truth, pouring out the oil of love as my worship to You. In surrender I must give my every part.' ('I will offer up my life', Matt Redman)	A song of self-sacrifice in God's service – with reminders of Jesus in conversation with a woman at a well, and his being anointed by another woman in a home.
'In your kingdom broken lives are made new, you make all things new.' ('Praise is rising', Benton Brown)	This whole song is about the hope of healing and renewal.

At the time of writing, in the CCLI top 25 there was a paucity of lyrics referencing the unity of believers in Jesus. This may be a temporary phenomenon – many will remember 'Bind us together' (Bob Gillman) from the 1970s!

Words from the Bible often make up our prayers and songs, and scripture thus enters our consciousness by a kind of back door. New Christians don't always realize where familiar texts come from, and may be pleasantly surprised to discover the cry, 'Holy, holy, holy!' in Isaiah 6 and again in Revelation 4, or to come across the familiar words of the Grace at the end of 2 Corinthians.

Non-biblical imagery and ideas in prayers and songs can add some spice to the mix and provoke us to think of God in new ways. Consider for example:

- Augustine's 'our hearts are restless until they rest in you', in the CW collect for the Seventeenth Sunday after Trinity;
- the idea of Jesus as 'Lord of the Dance' in Sydney Carter's song;
- Teresa of Avila's 'Nothing can trouble' in a Taizé chant;
- Jesus as 'the wind in these sails' in the song 'Jesus be the centre' by Michael Frye.

Not all such imagery is welcomed or helpful. Many people scorn the hymn 'God of concrete, God of steel' (Frederick R. C. Clarke and Richard Granville Jones, 1964) because of its harsh-sounding first line; but are they missing helpful insights in the rest of the hymn? Others are troubled by words with unhelpful connotations with regard to gender, race, disability or hierarchy.

TO DISCUSS

- In what ways have you seen people's lives change as they have grown in their faith?
- Do you think there is a problem with some parts of the Bible being neglected or difficult topics not handled?
- Share your favourite hymns or songs: do they include any reference to transformation?

FOR THE WIDER CHURCH

- What images would you want writers of new songs to include?
- As we look ahead to the future of worship, what are the limits on non-biblical imagery?

Actions that speak louder than words

If the words we say or sing shape the people that we are, surely our actions shape us all the more? These actions could be the postures that we adopt for prayer: do some congregations need to rediscover kneeling, or standing with raised hands? They could be the ritual acts of sharing a sign of God's peace, or eating and drinking Communion. They could be the simple welcome that we afford to unknown visitors who find their way into our churches – some visitors being like us, and others being unlike. (See C1 Sacramental.)

Our actions in church should shape us and prepare us for our actions outside.

Sent out for what?

We do not want to be 'so heavenly minded that we are no earthly good'. As we gaze upon Jesus, we become more like Jesus. The rhythm of our worship should include slower or quieter times when there are opportunities for God's still, small voice to be heard and heeded. As we become more like Jesus, our behaviour becomes more like his. And it is to live in so transformed a manner that we are sent on our way.

When we craft liturgies and songs for the future we should make sure that our worship (said, sung and symbolic) features both the dynamic character of Christ, which is not just 'beautiful' or 'wonderful' but caring, loving, leading, struggling, confronting; and also encouragement to the worshippers to become his disciples, Christ-like, active in the world on his behalf.

D2

CROSSING THRESHOLDS

In this chapter we will use some observations drawn from the study of anthropology to cast further light on how worship can help us become more like Jesus; he who is, of course, at the centre of our worship. (See the previous chapter, D1 To Become More Like Jesus, which deals more closely with the scriptural background.)

Public worship is a meeting place for the people of God with their Lord. It also offers a space of encounter for those who feel distant from God like strangers. Sunday and weekday worship, occasional offices and initiation services each offer their invitations into God's presence. True encounter with God leads to transformation and renewal. This should be as true of the disciple whose life is shaped by patterns of daily prayer and weekly worship as it is for the wedding couple who declare their undying love for one another in the heightened significance of a single great public act. They leave the church in a dramatically different relationship to each other and society from that in which they entered the church.

When people are transformed by God in the course of worship, they inevitably go out somehow different from the way they came in. So, when members of a congregation regularly recommit themselves to living in a Christ-like way through breaking bread and drinking wine they leave with the words, 'Go in peace to love and serve the Lord!' ringing in their ears. The Sending Out is not simply a conclusion but a missional commission to live in the light of that commitment made in communion with Christ. And when a couple take one another until death do them part within the love of God – Father, Son and Holy Spirit – then the same dynamic is at play. The congregation does not just bid them a happy life together but prays that their love may overflow to neighbours in need and embrace those in distress. If the vows were a response to the word of God, then the prayers play a part in the sending out.

 'Go therefore and make disciples of all nations, baptizing them in the name of the Father and of the Son and of the Holy Spirit, and teaching them to obey everything that I have commanded you. And remember, I am with you always, to the end of the age.' (Matt. 28.19–20)

Patterns of Christian worship, as they have emerged from the religious milieu of Jesus' times and have developed within human cultures and societies since, are the repository of a great deal of wisdom about human spiritual need and development. This includes the development of a religious language spoken through song, the poetry of words, symbol and ritual that can speak heavenly truth. It is not idealistic to say that worship can enable people to stand on the threshold between heaven and earth. In the Church's annual invitation for Christian people to enter into the events of the Passion narratives in Holy Week, or in its invitation to respond to the gospel as a regular part of worship, people are given the space and means to be identified with Christ in real, tangible and transformative ways. But this it not something confined to the moment of worship. Once you have allowed God to touch and change you, you must then go and live in the light of it.

TO THINK ABOUT

• How do you experience worship changing you?

TO DISCUSS

• Does your worship seem as if you are on the threshold of heaven and earth?

- How do you see others changed through worship, whether regular or occasional?

We are all spiritual beings

These patterns are also deeply embedded in our society. To some extent they spring out of the spiritual hard-wiring of human beings and come to life in worship. While the regular worship of the church provides space in which Christian people can find transformation through greater identity with Christ and his gospel, those who encounter it only occasionally are most likely to do so at moments of significant transition in their own lives. Victor Turner (1920–83) has described how people negotiate transitions in their lives through ritual from an anthropologist's perspective.[147] His research is based on work with very primitive societies and builds on van Gennep's threefold model for rites of passage.[148]

The lessons learned from the primitive societies that these anthropologists lived among shine a light on our own spiritual nature and our response to the knowledge we have of Jesus. Turner spots two elements that he regards as having vitality in marking spiritual transition in people's lives: *liminality* and *communitas*.

Liminality

Limen is the word for 'threshold' in Latin and is used by van Gennep as a metaphor for being 'betwixt and between'. He observes that the process of personal, spiritual and social tran-

147 Victor Turner, *The Ritual Process: Structure and Anti-structure*, Aldine Publishing, 1969; and Victor Turner, *The Forest of Symbols*, Cornell University Press, 1967.

148 A. van Gennep, *The Rites of Passage*, Routledge & Kegan Paul, 1960; For an analysis of the Eucharist seen through Van Gennep's lens see also Phillip Tovey, *Inculturation of Christian Worship: Exploring the Eucharist*, Ashgate Publishing, 2004; and Max Gluckman's approach to social process in *Rituals of Rebellion in South East Africa*, Manchester University Press, 1954.

sition can be expected to have these three phases: pre-liminal, liminal and post-liminal. It is not difficult to see this reflected in Christian worship. Many of the rites of *Common Worship* bear the marks of a fourfold pattern:

- Gathering.
- Reading of the Word.
- Response.
- Sending out.

It is in the Response that we cross the *limen*. In a Communion Service this may begin with sharing the Peace and will include taking bread and wine as we pray to be more like Jesus; in a wedding it may be the vows, the declaration and the kiss; in a service of praise and prayer this may be the sermon and the response or commitment that worshippers are invited to make; it is a moment of healing, of penitence, of conversion. And it is by the crossing of this threshold that we leave worship to live life in a new way. Worship before the *limen* is crossed is pre-liminal and worship that follows is the post-liminal phase.

Community

For Turner, 'community', or preferably '*communitas*' (a word less likely to be laced with non-technical meanings that can confuse his intention), is a further key to understanding how religious transformation is negotiated. He defines *communitas* as a perfect manifestation of community:

> ... the being no longer side by side (and, one might add, above and below) but with one another of a multitude of persons.[149]

He also sees *communitas* invariably in *liminality*. He argues that where people are on the threshold of transformation in a ritual setting alongside others, then a sense of ideal community often

---

149 Victor Turner, 'The Ritual Process', in Lambek (ed.), *Anthropology of Religion*, p. 372, quoting Martin Buber, 1961.

prevails. *Communitas* is subversive and transforming toward the prevailing society. He says, '...in Rites de Passages, men are released from structure into *communitas* only to return to structure revitalised by their experience of *communitas*'.[150]

This wisdom of the ages revealed here, not intellectualized but belonging to our inherited spiritual make-up, is betrayed in our need to gather for public worship and at moments of transition in people's lives. Indeed, God can bring change to an individual, as was the case for Paul on the Damascus road or Charles Wesley in his metaphorical dungeon. But it is in the act of gathering with others that this is cemented into our social make-up and we are enabled to live as people transformed by God in the world in a new way. (See the tables in D1 To Become More Like Jesus look at a number of other examples of promoting change in liturgy and hymnody.)

> Ananias laid his hands on Saul and said, 'Brother Saul, the Lord Jesus, who appeared to you on your way here, has sent me so that you may regain your sight and be filled with the Holy Spirit.' And immediately something like scales fell from his eyes, and his sight was restored. Then he got up and was baptized. (Acts 9.17–18)

None of this should be surprising to those whose spirituality is formed in the evangelical tradition. The essential place of conversion is understood not just in the head but in the hearts of those for whom this has been their experience. And the *limen* of conversion without the prayers and fellowship of the Christian *communitas* is a lonely and unsustainable place. We walk this way most emphatically in the company of others. Of course conversion may not be one great leap over a single significant hurdle. It is also negotiated in the repeated little transformations of those who return continually to the call of God through word and sacrament where they encounter again and again the *communitas* and a *limen*.

---

150 Victor Turner, 'The Ritual Process', p. 373.

Our vision for worship is extended as we realize the importance of our gatherings, in accompanying one another on the journey of faith and in the transformation to Christlikeness that the gospel calls us to.

TO DISCUSS

• What can you do in your church to enable people to be more aware they are in the company of others?
• Share some ideas to help people in worship to support one another to change and grow as disciples.

Christian worship today

When I look at your heavens, the work of your fingers,
the moon and the stars that you have established;
what are human beings that you are mindful of them,
mortals that you care for them.
(Ps. 8.3–4)

This brief reflection on the spiritual nature of all people, every one created by God, serves to highlight the importance of public worship for human flourishing and gospel transformation. While some may describe worship as a peculiarly religious thing to do, it may more properly be seen as an essentially human thing to do. It is when the church gathers together, its members consciously in the company of others, that they are called to spiritual change, attendant on the word of God, responding to that and sent back into the world, to become more nearly the people that the creator God would have them be. And here are real missional challenges and opportunities for our churches. This is a lens we can use again to look at the patterns of worship and its shaping of people's lives.

In the lives of the faithful

We can perhaps discern four rhythms of worship constantly in play and underlying one another:

- Daily prayer through morning, evening and night, in public and in personal quiet times.
- The regular rhythm of Sunday worship when the church community gathers together.
- The annual cycle of the Christian year punctuated strongly by Christmas and Easter through which we can enter into the good news of Jesus' birth, life, death and resurrection, and reflect on significant theological truths.
- The shape of our lives and our rites of passage from birth to death.

Christian people are likely to intertwine all four of these in their life's pattern. But the first two are distinctive to those who have an explicit and committed faith, while the last two have some force also across societies built on a Christian heritage but where faith has lapsed and is present only in the background. The first two also follow a rhythm that has a quicker pace than the annual and lifelong observance.

In the daily and weekly beat, a sense of *communitas* may be stronger in the fellowship of the church, but it is harder to discern the *limen*. What threshold do regularly worshipping communities cross each time they meet? Odo Casel opened up a new world of understanding about worship when he pointed out that here contemporary Christians transcend time and are brought into contact with the transforming presence of Christ.[151]

We can see the reality of this for instance in the regular reading of the Bible, in personal quiet times and daily prayer. The traditional liturgies of Morning Prayer, Evening Prayer and Compline give resonance with the time of the day in the regular reading of three Gospel poems (*Benedictus*, Luke 1.68–79, *Magnificat*, Luke 1.46–55 and *Nunc Dimittis*, Luke 2.29–32) that ring with

---

151 Odo Casel OSB (1886–1948), *The Mystery of Christian Worship*, Crossroads Publishing Company, 1999.

And you, child, will be called the prophet of the Most High; for you will go before the Lord to prepare his ways. (Luke 1.76)

The Mighty One has done great things for me, and holy is his name. (Luke 1.49)

Master, now you are dismissing your servant in peace, according to your word; for my eyes have seen your salvation. (Luke 2.29–30)

hope, realization and fulfilment respectively. Whether through personal quiet times or in shared liturgical prayer the story of Christ is daily brought into our experience of life. These are *liminal* places in which we cross a little threshold every day and form our own lives around Christ's. Transformation is perhaps difficult to discern day after day but, like the slow ascent of a helix, once we have gone around many times we are no longer in quite the same place as we were.

In the structure of *Common Worship* we can discern more easily the fourfold shape that encourages worshippers into a transformative encounter with God. Liturgy cannot make such an encounter inevitable, but it can help.

- Gathering in the light of life's joys and failures in praise and in confession.
- Reflecting on the word of God and discerning where it is leading us.
- Responding by prayer or sacrament or act of commitment, perhaps around Eucharist or wholeness and healing or discipleship and confirmation.
- The sending out of the witnessing and missional community.

And we can recognize the *limen* somewhere clearly in the Response. Not everybody may dare cross this threshold, but it is there, and those who will are invited to do so.

On the boundary between society and Church

In the Church of England context the rite of Infant Baptism sits in a very strange place. It both belongs to the Church with its committed faithful as an act of initiation and incorporation, while at the same time belonging to society as a rite of passage with a more inchoate form of prayer for a child's spiritual, relational and material wellbeing. It is neither fully an initiation into the community of the faithful nor is it a pastoral or occasional office. There can be little surprise that while this is unresolved baptism becomes a source of some considerable tension. (See C2 Baptismal.)

This is not the place to explore baptism policy, but the nature of the threshold that is crossed at the font merits a little consideration. The *Common Worship* context for the act of baptism is the same fourfold structure we are already familiar with.

- Gathering with thanks and in prayer for God's guidance.
- Considering the word of God including the Gospel.
- Responding by 'Decision' and in prayer for identification with the archetypal saving acts of God witnessed in the unfolding of God's revelation through Noah, Moses, John the Baptist and Jesus. Water principally makes this tangible.
- Sending out with a strong commission and prayer to live in the light of the hope of salvation.

It is of course quite possible to do all this without crossing any threshold at all. The threshold that is crossed is surely not found in the pouring of water but in identification with Christ – the beginning of walking his way. The worshipping community must surely do all it can to accompany those who come and are brought for baptism. A church that does not itself know what it means to be as Christ to others will be ill-equipped to do so. The problem with making baptism real may be less in the intention of the families who bring their children to the font than it is in the church unused to being at the threshold of the presence of God.

The vision of worship that is opened up by considering the journey of faith as one of transition and transformation has baptism at its centre. Here the church surrounds, accompanies and prays for those passing through the waters of death to new life.

In society at large

Here the two slowest beats of the rhythms of worship stand out: one marking the seasons of the year and the other the seasons of life. In the latter the features of *limen* and *communitas* are clear. The community gathered around a grieving spouse or two joyous newlyweds are clearly visible at a moment of dramatic change. Those who go into the church come out undoubtedly changed in relation to one another, in relation to society and in relation to God. And perhaps they come to the church in the first place because here is a place that houses a community that should know what it means to negotiate such deep, personal, relational and spiritual changes. It may be that a day when you arrive at the church gates a single person and leave bound to somebody else by substantial promises fills you with fear. It is undoubtedly the case that the day when you arrive with the mortal remains of a loved and cherished person and leave without them is a fearful thing. Crossing such thresholds demands the perspective of creatures who recognize the immensity of their creator. And doing this in the company of others who live with this perspective every day must surely help us make sense of God.

 Alongside events like weddings and funerals there are *liminal* crossings we have lost too. Dave Murrow regrets the loss of an adolescent rite, pointing out that in Islam and Mormonism young adolescent men are accompanied into manhood much more successfully.[152]

Confirmation no longer contains this for many good reasons and there is no Bar Mitzvah in the Christian Church. To some in contemporary society passing the driving test has become the pre-eminent adolescent rite.

---

152 http://churchformen.com/boyz-to-men/

There is a danger that an approach to worship born out of the study of human society causes us to over-analyse a mystery, but these things are perhaps clear:

- That God calls us to conversion and amendment of life.
- That this is worked out both in dramatic ways and in the small details of every single day.
- That we are not called to walk Christ's way alone but in the company of others.
- That we are only equipped to accompany others across their thresholds as we allow God to transform our lives too. It is only a transformed church that can be the agent of transformation in others. As the faithful are called through the patterns of prayer and worship to change, so their ministry of healing and pastoral care and initiation, and proclamation of Jesus' birth, life, death and resurrection is transformed too.
- But then it is perhaps simply too obvious to say that the people of God should attend to one another and to the *liminality* of their relationship with God if they are to grow and make a difference to the world.

Evangelistic opportunities

There are many moments of change that we must negotiate from time to time throughout our lives. They are not always immediately obvious as transitions through which we may be drawn closer to God, but remember how people are much more aware of the presence of God at *liminal* moments. Moving house or retirement are rarely noticed by the church – but perhaps they should be.

TO DISCUSS

- What could ministry to people retiring look like? Might this have both pastoral and evangelistic dimensions? Should prayer and worship be a part of this? Is it worthwhile considering an annual act of worship during which the newly retired can mark this transition?

- Many communities will see large housing developments spring up on their doorsteps over the next decade. Everybody who moves in to such new houses will be crossing a set of significant thresholds: forming new families, first home, new job, new neighbours, new landscape in which to live, new furniture, and so on. It would be easy for the local church to see the incomers as a nuisance. Are there ways in which they can be given the opportunity to mark their transitions through prayer and worship and ask of God to bless their futures?

- And then there are thresholds crossed in more obviously communal ways: the start of the year in a nursery or school with a new intake or leaving at the end of the year, mayor making, local tragedy and disaster such as experienced by Liverpudlians in Hillsborough, or even the peculiar reinterment of a king whose remains were found under a car park in Leicester. The last two demonstrate powerfully the need felt by a local community to come before God at moments when they are confronted by life's story, human failure, mortality and change. We might expect this to be no different at other times too if we can develop our sensitivity to what those around us are dealing with and facing.

D3

WORSHIP, MISSION AND
PASTORAL CARE

The development of pioneer ministry, Bishops' Mission Orders and sundry forms of Fresh Expressions of Church run the risk of encouraging the idea that 'traditional' church is focused on pastoral care and that we can leave evangelism to 'network' churches. Similarly, the concept of Fresh Expressions can slip into being so mission focused that it does not have space for pastoral care or even nurture. In both settings, worship should play an important role but can become a mere tool for evangelism in Fresh Expressions or be played safe so as not to offend anyone in traditional expressions of church. Note that all this is a caricature of both traditional and Fresh Expressions churches but, like all caricatures, it is rather too close to the truth for comfort.

There is a very traditional model of being Church that inter-relates all three dimensions: worship, mission and pastoral care. A recovery of this model serves both traditional and Fresh Expressions churches well. *On the Way*, a 1995 Church of England report drafted largely by Michael Vasey, attempted something like this. The most direct outcome of this report is in the CW Initiation Services 'Rites on the Way: Approaching Baptism'.[153]

The General Synod report on Intentional Evangelism (GS1917)[154] hints at this but does not mention any of the resources that already exist.

---

153 CWCI, pp. 15–56.
154 *Challenges for the Quinquennium: Intentional Evangelism*, General Synod of the Church of England, 2013.

Worship and mission

 In recent history it is possible to discern three broad models that describe the relationship between worship and mission:[155]

First, worship is what the faithful do and so all mission (especially evangelism) takes place away from acts of worship. Evangelism may be seen as a means of producing more worshippers and worship empowers people to go and do mission. In this model, where worship and mission are separate, pastoral need belongs in worship (where worship is a respite from a hard life). Pastoral need is a dimension of mission if this is conceived more broadly than simply as evangelism and includes significant elements of meeting human need.

Second, worship is a subset of mission/evangelism so that all worship is aimed at the seeker. Worship may become didactic and simply a vehicle for encouraging the congregation to repent, commit to faith or to sign up for a good cause such as a campaign for justice. Worship may cease to be worship when it focuses on God in a secondary way in that God is the object of the commitment to which the congregation is called. This approach tends to be individualistic and loses focus on the corporate nature of worship.

Third, worship is the primary locus for proclaiming the gospel and therefore is mission. John Wesley thought Holy Communion was a converting ordinance. He observed that in attending this service (the Book of Common Prayer version of course) we are presented with a clear exposition of justification by grace alone through faith. Gregory Dix thought the BCP Eucharist was the best liturgical vehicle ever devised to embody this doctrine. However, there is more to this than mere intellectual grasping of a doctrine. Wesley believed that in the Eucharist we are brought face to face with the prevenient grace of God which calls for a response from us. Thus this model is experiential. This model

---

155 See Thomas Schattauer, *Inside Out*, and Ruth Meyers in *Anglican Theological Review*. A more sustained treatment can be found in Ruth A. Meyers, *Missional Worship: Worshipful Mission*, Eerdmanns, 2014.

has been championed among North American (mainly Lutheran) liturgists – chiefly Frank Senn and Gordon Lathrop.[156] While this model coheres with the model we encourage, it can be used in a sloppy way, so failing to scrutinize and check that acts of worship are indeed functioning as expressions of the gospel.

> But experience shows the gross falsehood of that assertion, that the Lord's Supper is not a converting ordinance. Ye are witnesses. For many now present know, the very beginning of your conversion to God (perhaps, in some the first deep conviction) was wrought at the Lord's Supper.[157]

Pastoral care

Pastoral care is often automatically conceived in a therapeutic manner as helping people in need. However, there are other models that are sometimes more appropriate. If a basic aim of pastoral care is to see individuals and communities flourish, then sometimes this needs attitudes and behaviour to be challenged. Hence pastoral care may take the form of confronting people and groups with uncomfortable truths about themselves and may also entail defending the oppressed, speaking for those who are being ignored, exposing the self-obsessed and so on. These models of pastoral care may be termed 'challenge' or 'prophetic' models.

Pastoral care and mission connect with each other in a variety of ways. Many would say that the best way to care for someone is to introduce them to Jesus. Justin Welby speaks of how, shortly after becoming Archbishop of Canterbury, he was in a meeting with a very senior member of the Cabinet. They could

---

156 Frank Senn, *The Witness of the Worshiping Community: Liturgy and the Practice of Evangelism*, Paulist Press, 1993; Frank Senn, with Mark Olson and Jann Fullenwieder, *How Does Worship Evangelize?*, Augsburg Fortress, 1995; Gordon Lathrop, *Holy Things: A Liturgical Theology*, Fortress Press, 1993; *Holy People: A Liturgical Ecclesiology*, Fortress Press, 1999; and *Holy Ground: A Liturgical Cosmology*, Fortress Press, 2009.

157 John Wesley, *Journal*, 27–28 June 1740.

not agree on the matter they were discussing, so hoping to find at least some measure of agreement somewhere, the Minister of State said, 'Well, at least we can agree that the Church is here to do good.' The archbishop replied: 'Well no, primarily we are here to talk about Jesus and introduce people to him.' Of course, part of Christian discipleship is to do good (and to seek justice) but it is important to see where this fits. Amos 5 shows that if we do not seek justice, our worship is false. In other words, actions are the test of authentic worship. William Temple put it like this: 'People are always thinking that conduct is supremely important, and that because prayer helps it, therefore prayer is good. That is true as far as it goes; still truer is it to say that worship is of supreme importance and conduct tests it.'

> I hate, I despise your festivals,
> and I take no delight in your solemn assemblies.
> Even though you offer me your burnt offerings and grain
>   offerings,
> I will not accept them;
> and the offerings of well-being of your fatted animals
> I will not look upon.
> Take away from me the noise of your songs;
> I will not listen to the melody of your harps.
> But let justice roll down like waters,
> and righteousness like an ever-flowing stream.
> (Amos 5.21–24)

Mission which focuses on working for justice and peace is pastoral care in that God's Church seeks thereby to make life better for people – meeting human need. This may be by giving a helping hand (e.g. by running a foodbank) or challenging the injustice that makes the helping hand necessary (e.g. by pointing out that national policy leads to the need for foodbanks). Most of the time, of course, the Church cannot 'make it better' but is also called to accompany people in their pain and difficulty. This too is mission and pastoral care joined together.

Worship is pastoral care when it carries the message of new life and forgiveness. It speaks of a God of justice who is both comfort (to the congregation) and challenge (to the society in which we live) in an unjust world. The challenge is presented here to individuals and congregations alike – perhaps penitential rites embody this most clearly.

Worship, mission and the kingdom of God

In *The Church in the Power of the Spirit*, Jürgen Moltmann suggests that an act of worship should be disturbing.[158] While many of us have been to services that disturbed us for all the wrong reasons, what he is getting at is that in worship we catch a vision of the kingdom of God and realize that the world is not in reality how it should be. We are compelled therefore to go out from worship fired up to change the world for God, to live out the kingdom and to be God's people for God's world. This looks similar to Shattauer's first model and so is open to the critique that it can make worship functional by being merely a resource for mission. But Moltmann's mandate is more completely fulfilled within a model of 'worship as mission'. Here worship is seen as a glimpse of heaven, a foretaste of life in the new Jerusalem. This may sometimes be a rather romantic view of worship as most services are not like this, yet they do contain flashes of encounter with God when this kind of vision shines through.

Rites on the Way

There are many good ideas buried in Church of England reports. In 1995 the House of Bishops' Report *On the Way* brought together a review of patterns for Christian initiation, for both adults and children (including the age of admission to Communion), the need for a rite of adult commitment, and an evaluation of the ancient practice of the catechumenate, together with work on Christian formation, ethics, evangelism and discipleship in the light of evangelism and nurture courses, such as Alpha, and

---

158 Jürgen Moltmann, *The Church in the Power of the Spirit*, SCM Press, 1977.

various Christian Basics courses. Developments in all these areas had been happening in isolation from each other.

TO THINK ABOUT

- What might joined-up thinking in these areas look like today?

> Go therefore and make disciples of all nations, baptizing them in the name of the Father, and of the Son and of the Holy Spirit, and teaching them to obey everything that I have commanded you. And remember, I am with you always, to the end of the age. (Matt. 28.19–20)

The baptism and confirmation texts that then emerged in *Common Worship* had a stronger focus on mission than the ASB texts did. In the intervening years not all nurture courses have linked in with liturgy and the 2015 Church of England report on discipleship (GS1977) did not seem aware of the previous report. A set of resources called *Rites on the Way* was produced in 2006. Michael Vasey had begun to write these when he died in 1998 and the Liturgical Commission eventually finished them and published them. They have not been widely publicized and deserve greater use. They include prayers to welcome people who wish to learn about the Christian faith (and the notes make clear this does not have new enquirers in view but people at a stage or two further on). There is also material for 'The Presentation of the Four Texts'. This refers back to an attempt a few years ago to identify a small core of texts which all Anglicans might be expected to know. The four texts are:

- Jesus' summary of the Law.
- The Lord's Prayer.
- The Apostles' Creed.
- The Beatitudes.

Rites on the Way[159] is a resource that attempts to link liturgy with mission in terms of nurture but undoubtedly much more could be done here. What is not really evident is a link with mission in terms of social action, though the baptism texts do point to baptism being the beginning of a life of discipleship.

Making it real in practice

The problem is not grasping the idea of relating worship, mission and pastoral care together. It is seeing how it might happen in practice. Here are seven ideas.

- Consider the topics that appear in the intercessions. Michael Vasey wrote in 1988: 'Picture a Rite A Parish Communion in a suburban congregation and imagine the biddings at the intercessions. There is unlikely to be an echo of much day to day experience possibly shared by the congregation: gossip, mortgages, advertising, adultery, supermarkets, travel, diocesan quota, or evangelism. Sickness is defined in medical terms, mental anguish and death are probably out of sight. God's function is to bring peace and health in the personal and domestic sphere and to preserve the present social order if that turns out to be within his power.'[160] But in reality some churches have abandoned intercessions as part of their regular worship. Ruth Meyers found a dearth of intercessory prayer while visiting a wide variety of churches on her sabbatical.[161] It is worth analysing your intercessions to see what gets prayed for and what is left out. (See also C5 Intercessory.)
- Some churches interview members of the congregation as part of the service and ask, 'What will you be doing this time tomorrow?' This too can lead into intercession, but it could also be a springboard for praise for the gifts God gives to people.

---

159 See CW: *Rites on the Way*, Church House Publishing, 2012.
160 Michael Vasey, *Intercessions in Worship*, GBW 77, 1988.
161 Ruth Meyers, *Missional Worship*, 2014.

- You can insert references to God's justice and care into the Eucharistic Prayer (*Common Worship* makes space for locally written prefaces to Eucharistic Prayers A, B and E and the Alternative Eucharistic Prayer One).
- You could organize an event that celebrated people's work and hobbies. A display in church could form the backdrop for a service (or part of a service) celebrating this.
- Brighton churches organize an Advent beach hut event. Each evening in Advent, a different beach hut opens up to reveal a suitable Advent scene. There is a short service and on Christmas Eve 24 beach huts open with a suitable Advent service to conclude the beach hut project. In Ripon, they hold an angel festival in the town organized by the churches and including acts of worship.[162]
- In a parish suffering from a lot of problems with street crime, burnt-out cars and burglary the church wrote a prayer for the protection of the parish which was used as a collect in every service and which they encouraged people to pray daily at home.
- You can encourage traditional open-air worship events such as Good Friday acts of witness or Christmas carols at a civic Christmas tree. Alternatively congregations can come out of church into the street if a touring sports event is passing their door such as a marathon or the Tour de France.

TO DISCUSS

- What could your church do in the coming year to bring the world into your worship or take your worship into the world?
- How is societal life and a vision for God's kingdom represented in the intercessions of your church?

TO THINK ABOUT

- In the Prayers of Penitence, what sorts of things get confessed?

---

162 Mark Tanner, *City of Angels*, GBEv 104.

D4

PROPHETIC

Perhaps the most famous reported prophecy in recent years is that of Dr S. M. Lockeridge (1913–2000), Pastor of Calvary Baptist Church in San Diego, California, and supporter of Martin Luther King's non-violent stand against racial inequality. Lockeridge spoke for six and half minutes with no notes and no prior warning – he just opened his mouth and God gave him the words to exalt Jesus. The prophetic message of 'That's my King!' (readily available on YouTube) still stands: Do you know him? And, if so, what difference will it make? Do we have a dream today which will bring transformation tomorrow?

The prophetic in worship and transforming mission to the world

Inspiring worship 'glorifies God and edifies the people' (Canon B1.2); it draws people into God's presence and grows the Church. There is no such thing as ordinary time! Each act of worship is a unique opportunity to encounter God, to grow in discipleship, but then to go back out into the world as salt and light to make a difference. We have already seen in earlier chapters that worship is about a transforming encounter with the living God and that this transformation should change character, challenge culture and in turn transform society. Kathy Galloway suggests: 'Churches need to be prophetic voices, reading the signs of the times in the light of the justice and love of God, and speaking out against all that distorts or diminishes the image of God in human beings ... This affects the way we pray and sing and share word and sacrament.'[163]

> You are the salt of the earth; but if salt has lost its taste, how can its saltiness be restored? ... You are the light of the world. A city built on a hill cannot be hid. No one after lighting a lamp puts it under the bushel basket, but on the lampstand, and it gives light to all in the house. In the same way, let your light shine before others, so that they may see your good works and give glory to your Father in heaven. (Matt. 5.13–16)

The Church's call to be a prophetic people should be forging the way in re-forming, re-shaping, re-visioning the Church through its worship. We speak to God; he speaks to us. This is a dynamic interaction enabling us to speak into situations, a church sent out from worship with a God-given, transforming mission to the world.

Basic definitions

'Defining prophecy is a notoriously difficult matter',[164] but we will attempt to do so, rooting our discussion biblically, theologically and liturgically. Prophecy means to forth tell or to proclaim. The Hebrew 'naba' means to speak under inspiration; to preach; to cry to; or to put forth; telling something that God has spontaneously brought to mind.[165] Prophecy does not mean foretell or predict, although an element of this may be involved, linked with the future destiny of an individual, a church or a particular situation. The opposite of prophecy is nostalgia: a wistful looking back; a sentimental longing for things, persons or situations that are past and irrevocable. However, if we focus only on the past or the future, we may miss what God wants to do now.

---

163 Kathy Galloway, in *Worship: Window of the Urban Church*, ed. Tim Stratford, SPCK, 2006, p. 13.

164 John Goldingay, *Old Testament Prophecy Today*, GB Renewal R1, 2003, p. 3.

165 Wayne Grudem, *Systematic Theology*, IVP, 1994.

Prophecy implies divine origin. Kittel suggests that the original root of 'nabi' involves 'speaking with frenzy' giving a sense of being overwhelmed by the divine presence. Prophets were often thought to be mad by others, but 'the prophet is never overwhelmed to such an extent as to degrade the personality of the prophet'.[166]

Here we find hints of the kind of experiential excesses that have at times brought spiritual gifts a bad press today. It is clear that the biblical prophets were not afraid to appear eccentric or offensive, but their call was constantly one to look outwards and right the wrongs of the world, to rebuke in order to bring hope. We will do well to follow their example to keep the focus off ourselves and on mission to the world.

God is looking for a prophetic people

In biblical terms, it is clear that God is looking for a prophetic people. In the Old Testament, Moses tells Joshua: 'I wish that all the Lord's people were prophets and that the Lord would put his Spirit on them!' (Num. 11.29). Later, Joel announces: 'In those days ... I will pour out my Spirit on all people. Your sons and daughters will prophesy' (Joel 2.28–32, also quoted by Peter on the day of Pentecost in Acts 2). In the New Testament, Paul encourages the church in Corinth to 'eagerly desire spiritual gifts, especially the gift of prophecy' (1 Cor. 14.1) and John exhorts 'anyone who has an ear to listen to what the Spirit is saying to the churches' (Rev. 2 and 3). This kind of prophecy is clearly different from those of the Old Testament prophets recorded in the canon of scripture, which alone stand with the divine authority of the written word of God. No details are given, although we can assume the intention of these spontaneous utterances was to 'prepare God's people for works of service, so that the body of Christ may be built up' (Eph. 4.12).

Jesus takes prophecy a stage further when he reads from Isaiah (Luke 4), claiming that 'Today this scripture has been fulfilled in

---

166 David Atkinson, *Prophecy*, GBW 49, 1977, p. 8. See also 1 Cor. 14.32.

your hearing'. This prophetic utterance was then worked out in quantifiable action with measurable fruit in the ministry of Jesus. It has also been a charge to the Church ever since. God speaks prophetically into society through the Church in order to preach good news to the poor, to bring release from oppression, and healing to the nations.

This has implications theologically. Dave Bilbrough points out, 'In an age where worship and the pursuit of new, fresh and high quality expressions abound, let's not allow ourselves to get trapped in a kind of Christian parallel universe that sees worship as a kind of fuzzy, warm "out of the body" experience to the detriment of an active participation and partnership with God to make a difference in this world.'[167]

Worship can feed and restore us, but it is not merely a 'spiritual fix' or the latest quest for a feel-good experience for a short time on a Sunday morning. This is counter-cultural in an individualistic consumerist society, which only looks to its own interests. Our true spiritual worship (Rom. 12.1) is to be offered sacrificially to God as we live out in the world from Monday to Saturday. And the true prophetic voice will speak out to bring about righteousness, equality and justice on behalf of those who have no voice, reflecting God's heart for the lost, the marginalized and the exploited. If we truly believe that the earth is the Lord's and everything in it (Ps. 24.1), then we will be mindful of this in both our worship and our responsibility to care for the world around us and the people who live in it. Indeed, there are stern words from the prophets Isaiah (chapter 58) and Amos (5.23–24) about behaviour in worship if it is not matched by our action outside the assembly. It is encouraging as we look back to find such life-changing social action as free education for all and the abolition of slavery during the nineteenth century and, more recently, the hospice movement all growing out of the worshipping Church.

Why do we fast, but you do not see?
Why humble ourselves, but you do not notice?

---

167 Dave Bilbrough, *Worship and Mission*, New Wine Press, 2006, p. 17.

Look, you serve your own interest on your fast day,
and oppress all your workers.
(Isa. 58.3)

Take away from me the noise of your songs;
I will not listen to the melody of your harps.
But let justice roll down like waters,
and righteousness like an ever-flowing stream.
(Amos 5.23–24)

Common Worship and the prophetic

In some ways, *Common Worship* itself could be described as prophetic. Its arrival on the scene in 2000 marked a major sea-change from one book to a whole library of liturgical resources and a new emphasis on the importance of structure within a service alongside greater opportunity for flexibility and creativity. In part this was a response by the Church of England's General Synod to bridge the gulf between the Church and ordinary people in the Urban Priority Areas begun with the publication of *Patterns for Worship*. Structure maintains the family likeness, but freedom of choice enables worship to become indigenous and to speak directly into the lives of its local community. A quick glance around the congregation can be illuminating: who gathers and what do they look like? A genuinely all-age congregation of mixed class and ethnicity is of itself a prophetic demonstration of the coming kingdom, where all will be equally loved and valued. (See A2 Caring and Inclusive.)

TO THINK ABOUT

- Within a service, the prophetic voice can be heard in many ways. Consider how you have encountered a challenge from God.

The prophetic voice in liturgy

For Anglicans the liturgy enshrines our identity and our doctrine, so it is important that authorized texts are respected. Alongside this, the rubrics frequently suggest, 'These or other suitable words may be used', giving the opportunity for alternatives. These can not only bring seasonal variation and choices from the *Common Worship* library, but can also enable the inclusion of liturgies from elsewhere to bring immediacy, directness, freshness and life. Furthermore, we can be counter-cultural in our use of liturgy, following the example of what Walter Brueggemann describes as 'liturgical resistance' in the worship of Israel, as they publicly voice pain, challenge established power and use song and dance as a gesture of defiance.[168]

Through our liturgy, we can publicly proclaim kingdom values and our hopes for the world. And if the words that we speak out and pray together (*lex orandi*) then become the laws of belief (*lex credendi*) that we live by, then we go back out into the community carrying the potential for wider transformation.

From the same instruction, it can be implied that these or other words might be omitted altogether. *Common Worship* has been criticized for being too wordy and the Church has been more broadly criticized for being locked in a word/mind culture when the world around has long since moved on.[169]

This is a pertinent reminder that the biblical prophets frequently 'saw pictures' or 'took symbolic action'. In a world of visual images and icons, how much more should we be drawing out the symbols of worship which accompany the liturgy and drawing on new ones to make connections and speak into our contemporary culture.

The prophetic voice in preaching

Through history, the prophetic voice has been closely associated with preaching, teaching and the proclamation of the word of

---

168 See Galloway, *Worship: Window of the Urban Church*, p. 13, 14.
169 See Peter Craig-Wild's *Tools for Transformation*, DLT, 2002, p. 20.

God. Through prayerful preparation and interaction with the scriptures, the preacher receives a 'word' from God to pass on to the people, usually accompanied by some explanation and application. At times, the preacher can appear to speak out God's thoughts in 'inverted commas', leading on into intercessory prayer, spiritual warfare or social action. Many can testify to occasions when the preacher seemed to be speaking directly to them and their situation, perhaps bringing conviction or challenge, encouragement or renewed hope. When they go out from worship, a change has occurred. (See C5 Intercessory.)

The Lectionary encourages us to read the Bible systematically and thus avoids a narrow diet of scripture or the avoidance of difficult texts. The possibility of departing from the published Lectionary during Ordinary Time allows a scheme of readings to speak more specifically into the place and times in which we find ourselves now, both as a church and as a wider society. More interactive sermons with opportunities for the congregation to participate and offer further insights may also give fresh opportunity for God to speak. (See B2 Biblical, box on the Lectionary, and D1 To Become More Like Jesus; Transformation through words of scripture.)

The prophetic voice in prayer

In the usual order of things, prayers of intercession are frequently placed close to the sermon, in which we are invited to hold the needs of the world before God. John Pritchard points out that there is deep human instinct to pray especially when in trouble but this brings with it a danger that God is treated as a celestial cash-point.

If we are really honest, we often don't know how to pray and it is then that the Holy Spirit intercedes

> The danger is that God is treated as a celestial cash-point who can be manipulated round to our way of thinking. However, at the heart of this instinct is the instinct to love.[170]

170 John Pritchard, *The Intercessions Handbook*, SPCK, 1997, pp. 6–7.

for us sometimes with groans that cannot be expressed in words (Rom. 8.26–27). What is more, we can be sure that the Holy Spirit prays in accordance with God's will. As we recognize what is on God's heart, then we often see situations from a different perspective which in turn leads us into more meaningful prayer. We find out what God is doing and we are invited to join in! A crucial corollary of intercession is our willingness to be part of the answer to our own prayers.

Jesus taught his disciples how to pray using the words of the Lord's Prayer, including the words: 'your kingdom come, your will be done, on earth as in heaven'. This in itself is a prophetic proclamation of things yet to come.

The prophetic voice in silence

There are some who think prayer is what starts when the words stop! In Old Testament times, the 'word' (of the Lord) came to Jeremiah at the end of a time of prayer and careful listening, and Elijah heard the voice of God in that silent space after the earthquake, wind and fire. A closeness and attentiveness to God is basic to the prophetic function. (See C7 Silence.)

Throughout *Common Worship*, the liturgy is punctuated with the rubric, 'Silence is kept', but how often does this really happen? We should avoid the temptation to overfill our services to such an extent that God is always waiting in the wings but never given an opportunity to make an entry. If we do not spend time quietly listening, how can we learn to recognize God's voice?

Periods of silence may be kept at different points of the service. It may be particularly appropriate at the beginning of the service, after the readings and the sermon, and during the prayers.[171]

---

171 CW, *A Service of the Word*, p. 26, Note 4.

The prophetic voice in song

Although some hymns and songs stand the test of time, many come and go. This has always been the case, as the content of songs prophetically communicates what God is saying and doing in the Church 'now'. New moves of God produce new expressions of worship. Thus we find the composer J. S. Bach, responding to the Reformation with chorales in the vernacular and the advent of Methodism accompanied by a wealth of Wesley hymns. The path of spiritual song during the latter half of the twentieth century is helpfully charted by Pete Ward in his book, *Selling Worship*, which is subtitled 'How what we sing has changed the church'.[172]

The song of the Church has moved from teaching to dynamic encounter in the 1960s and 70s, through the public proclamation and witness of praise marches to intimacy in worship in the 1980s and 90s. And if Soul Survivor brought us back to the heart of worship, then the songs of John Bell and others have drawn out a new interest in psalms of lament and songs of justice, which reflect God's heart of compassion for a broken world. (See C8 Musical.)

It is also true that God frequently speaks within the context of sung worship. Music can be a stimulus to prophecy as we see in scripture when Elisha asked for a harpist to help him 'tune in' to God, who then spoke through Elisha (2 Kings 3.15). Music can be a powerful vehicle for the prophetic, but there are dangers. Although clearly God works through our emotions, we must not confuse an emotional response to the music with the presence of God. We must learn to discern the difference.

Beyond *Common Worship*

Neither *Common Worship* nor any liturgical successor will ever be the last word in worship. The Church has fixed forms for good theological and doctrinal reasons, but these should not

---

172 Authentic Media, 2005.

squeeze out the prophetic, the spontaneous and the unpredictable work of the Holy Spirit.

Mark Earey observes that the *Mission-shaped Church* report has led to subsequent adaptation of the structures of the Church, particularly as it impacts on the parochial system, with the establishment of Bishops' Mission Orders and a 'principled and careful loosening of the structures' (as Archbishop Rowan Williams called it in the General Synod debate of 2004). What is interesting is that there has been no suggestion of a parallel 'principled and careful loosening' or adaptation of the liturgical rules of the Church of England.[173]

Bishop Stephen Cottrell goes further and suggests that 'the eternal word which reorders all creation only speaks in local dialects'. Additional Collects, Additional Eucharistic Prayers and the Additional Baptism Texts in Accessible Language may be attempts to make language more readily accessible, but we may need to go further to develop liturgy and language that is truly indigenous.

TO DISCUSS

- Certainly our present plethora of liturgies has received much criticism for being too wordy. However, is this the fault of the liturgies themselves or does the problem lie with those preparing and leading worship?
- Share some ways in which the whole people of God can become fully involved rather than being passive consumers or spectators.

According to 1 Corinthians 14.26, we should all (not just those leading and preaching) come prepared with something to offer in worship. This should always be the case if liturgy is truly to be 'the work of the people'.

No one knows the mind of God, but together we have the potential to discern more of God's thoughts. Perhaps a decline

---

173 Mark Earey, *Beyond Common Worship*, SCM, 2013, pp. 54, 55.

in clergy numbers is actually a gift to the Church to mobilize and empower the laity in new and exciting ways.

Worship is so much more than words on a page. It is important to recognize that the Holy Spirit can be as active in the preparation and listening prayer beforehand as in the actual act of worship itself. The more time we spend with God, the more likely we are

Liturgy is often referred to as 'the work of the people' from its Greek derivation, meaning the whole people working together for the common good. In Greco-Roman terms, this was civil work such as building roads or aqueducts done by members of the populace to the highest standard to honour the emperor and for the benefit of all.

to hear and discern his prophetic word for today and how that might be communicated during the worship and preaching of a subsequent service.

Jonny Baker goes further still. Working in an alternative worship Fresh Expressions context, he introduces the idea of

curating worship [in order to] imagine new worlds, new relationships, new strategies and tactics, and counter-publics, about saying other worlds are possible, that business as usual in church, in worship, in theology, in consumer culture, in the world at large, in life, simply will not do.[174]

There is something deeply prophetic in this counter-cultural approach as it incarnates the gospel 'now' with directness and immediacy. It also demonstrates the implicit expectation that worship will have a transforming effect on participants, their networks in the surrounding neighbourhood and the wider world. (See also A5 Well-led.)

---

174 Jonny Baker, *Curating Worship*, SPCK, 2010, p. 10.

When the Spirit speaks

The 'evangelical awakenings' of the eighteenth and nineteenth centuries and the charismatic renewal of the twentieth century have firmly brought the work of the Holy Spirit and the prophetic back into the Church. This is prophecy on the level of 1 Corinthians 12—14 rather than prophecy in the canon of scripture. This in turn has raised our expectation that spiritual gifts will be exercised as part of the service on a regular basis, so how does this work out in practice? (See B5 Filled with the Spirit.)

Charismatic renewal has emphasized the importance of 'every member' ministry. God can speak through each of us if we are willing to hear his voice, but we will only prophesy in part (1 Cor. 13.12), coloured by personality and our own view of the world at that particular moment. We will need to prepare a congregation to participate by raising expectations and encouraging flexibility and spontaneity. We will also need to make room by paring back other elements within a service to create sufficient space to listen.

When God truly speaks, something that was not in existence at that point is brought into being. Thus, God said: 'Let there be light' at creation and there was light (Gen. 1.3); and God spoke to Abraham as the father of many nations even though he had no heir (Rom. 4.17). We have many biblical examples of the prophetic coming to the people of God through words, pictures, visions, dreams or symbolic actions. These are still all valid means of God speaking today, but they need to be offered with humility to strengthen, encourage and comfort (1 Cor. 14.3) and under the supervision of the leadership. People in the congregation need to know who is responsible for discerning whether this is from God or not and how it will be checked out. Prophecy should be written down, shared with others, studied, taken back to God in prayer, and then it should move us into action.

TO DISCUSS

- Where is there space in your church for members to share what God is saying to them?
- Where does your church's vision come from?

> Pursue love and strive for the spiritual gifts, and especially that you may prophesy. For those who speak in a tongue do not speak to other people but to God; for nobody understands them, since they are speaking mysteries in the Spirit. On the other hand, those who prophesy speak to other people for their upbuilding and encouragement and consolation. Those who speak in a tongue build up themselves, but those who prophesy build up the church. (1 Cor. 14.1–4)

Paul tells the Thessalonians not to treat prophecies with contempt but to test everything and hold on to the good (1 Thess. 5.19–21). Discernment, distinguishing of spirits and wisdom are often spiritual gifts missing from the Church today and yet they were those most highly valued by the Desert Fathers. We need to heed Kenneth Leech's warnings that there can be a fundamental irrationality and lack of theological and intellectual seriousness in assessing the charismatic.[175]

A 'word' should reveal something of God, his will for the church and his righteousness outworked within society; it is not a place to criticize the church or its leadership, prefaced by 'I, the Lord, say to you ...' or rounded up with 'Thus says the Lord', which set it six feet above contradiction. The need to test everything is a safeguard against spiritual mavericks who avoid accountability or try to draw attention to themselves and those seeking new spiritual experiences for their own sake.

Paul warns the Corinthians that if spiritual gifts are not exercised in love outworked in righteous and moral living, they are just meaningless, empty words (1 Cor. 13.1). When Isaiah met with God in worship, it led him to repentance and a new commission to go (Isa. 6). Indeed, we have much to learn from the

---

175 D. Bunch and A. Ritchie (eds), *Prayer and Prophecy: The Essential Kenneth Leech*, DLT, 2009, p. 47.

Roman Catholic slum priests, who 'pioneered ministries which lifted people out of the squalor of their surroundings and gave them the worth and dignity they had been denied almost everywhere else'.[176]

These priests went out from the Mass with a clear emphasis on the *missio dei* to transform their local communities. This is also true of many Fresh Expressions today, planted in places no one has wanted to go.

Looking to the future

We don't have to look far in the Gospels to discover that Jesus was forever upsetting regular worship in either the synagogue or Temple. This dynamic, Spirit-led, prophetic style of ministry has never sat easily within established patterns of worship. It can be disruptive and messy, but the opposite of order is not necessarily disorder. It can bring spontaneity, freedom, healing and transformation, and we may well need to loosen our structures further. The kind of Church with a prophetic edge will also be visionary, disturbing, incarnational and fruitful. We see a Church which is not an end in itself but a herald of God's coming kingdom giving us a glimpse of heaven on earth in our present time. As we release the prophetic within the Church, we go out into the world not only 'in peace to love and serve the Lord' but to see that which has not yet become a kingdom reality.

Prophecy takes us outside the church walls and into the world. Leech observes: 'Our society is largely alienated from spiritual values, but at the same time tolerates and even encourages ... pockets of spirituality, having reduced them to the status of hobbies.'[177] People are searching, so what will fill the spiritual vacuum? We have the potential to bring vision, give direction and release destiny.

---

176 Stephen Cottrell, in Steven Croft and Ian Mobsby (eds), *Fresh Expressions in the Sacramental Tradition*, Canterbury Press, 2009, p. 67.
177 Bunch and Ritchie, *Prayer and Prophecy*, p. 210.

D5

ESCHATOLOGICAL

Jesus said, 'I watched Satan fall from heaven like a flash of lightning. See, I have given you authority to tread on snakes and scorpions, and over all the power of the enemy; and nothing will hurt you. Nevertheless, do not rejoice at this, that the spirits submit to you, but rejoice that your names are written in heaven.' (Luke 10.18–20)

It may be that a deep change is taking place in the understanding of the evangelical branch of the Church about the eschatological nature of worship and Christian mission. The key message of the gospel, according to some evangelical church cultures, was the need of individuals to come to Jesus in repentance and faith to be saved by him so that one day they would get to heaven. While not wanting to lose this central importance of a personal response to the claims of Jesus Christ on the lives of individuals, we are seeing nowadays a broader picture. This idea of personal response and faith may be the central message of the gospel, but we are living in a time when we are increasingly seeing not just the centre but the edges as well.

4:3 vision

Your TV set today probably has a control on it for picture width. If you want to read the sub-titles on an old film you are watching you have to set it to 'centre cut-out' which means that you only get a 4:3 slice of the picture, with wide black margins at either side. But to reset it to 16:9 for a modern film means that you can suddenly see what's going on all the way across to the edges of the screen, rather than just in the middle section. In the past we have often watched the unfolding story of salvation in 4:3 ratio. We begin with the Fall and individual sin, see that sin taken to the cross by Jesus, and then we occasionally get a glimpse of the promise of the future heaven, peopled by all those who have been to the cross with Jesus and been given new life in him. But to switch the film to widescreen means that we can see more: the very early and the very last pages of our Bibles tell of a story which begins before time with creation, which God sees as very good, and which ends with new heavens and, significantly, a new earth. The broad sweep of God's purposes includes not just individuals making a personal profession of faith, but the renewal and renovation of the whole created order.

It is paradoxical that this new and wider vision of the gospel is making its presence felt at a time when our culture is as individualistic as it has ever been. But alongside the postmodern doctrine of individualism has come also a greater awareness of our connectedness to the created world, and, for Christians, a clearer vision that God is not only interested in gaining individual believers but rather in restoring all the universe to the status and wholeness he had always intended for it.

This widescreen view of the gospel changes everything. Churches are not just in the business of making new believers in Jesus Christ: we are now about working with him towards the renewal of all creation. Martin Luther apparently said, 'If I knew the world would perish tomorrow, I would still plant my apple tree today.' All that we do which is good and creative will last into eternity, so our task now is to do as much as we can which will last, which will have eternal significance. Our calling is to 'live in the direction' of the renewal of all things, living in such a way that we are doing the kind of things which God is doing as he prepares the universe for its recreation.

Our worship, therefore, ought to reflect this widescreen view of God's purposes. We celebrate creation as well as redemption; we call people not just to respond to Jesus but also to live for him; we seek to build up the world and not just the Church. Familiar texts take on new significance once we see this widescreen vision. We celebrate with bread and wine 'until he comes';

our affirmation that 'Christ will come again' (we may prefer the Church in Wales', 'Christ will come in glory') or our prayer, 'Lord Jesus, come in glory', take on new meanings; our looking 'for the coming of your kingdom' means so much more, and we look with new anticipation to the 'feast in heaven where all creation worships you'. In the meantime we 'work together for that day when your kingdom comes and justice and mercy will be seen in all the earth'. We also pray:

Bless the earth, heal the sick, let the oppressed go free
and fill your Church with power from on high ...
Gather your people from the ends of the earth
to feast with all your saints at the table in your kingdom,
where the new creation is brought to perfection
in Jesus Christ our Lord ...[178]

in faith that one day we will see
the vision of that eternal splendour for which you have
    created us.[179]

And of course our prayer at any and every act of worship asks that God's kingdom will come here on earth, as it is already being fulfilled in heaven.

Eschatological tension

But at a level deeper than mere texts, the eschatological dimension forces us, as we worship, to confront what Oscar Cullmann (1902–99) called 'eschatological tension', the fact that the kingdom has neither come in its fullness nor is it a future event for which we can only hope. This fact allows our worship to sit in the gap between triumphalism (wanting our triumph too early) and despair (giving up on triumph altogether). It explains why we struggle, why intercessions can seem a waste of breath as we pray again and again for the same trouble-spots, why testimonies

178 CW, Order One, Eucharistic Prayer F.
179 CW, Order One, Eucharistic Prayer G.

can seem empty and hollow to some while inspiring to others, why prayer or healing ministry can seem to be a waste of time, and why some worship-songs can take leave of any kind of reality. It opens up a rich seam for preaching more than mere platitudes to Christians who are genuinely struggling with the circumstances of their lives, but more significantly with why God appears to be doing so little.

While our *Common Worship* texts do much to remind us of the future glory awaiting us, there seems to be little which makes this tension and struggle explicit. Some hymnody does this well: the line, 'We feebly struggle; they in glory shine', catches this mood precisely, but this sentiment does not seem to be well reflected in the current texts. Of course we confess our sins at the start of most services, but there does not seem to be much nuance of our failing because we live in a fallen world awaiting renewal, rather than our failing because we are just, basically, useless sinners.

> O blest communion, fellowship divine!
> we feebly struggle, they in glory shine;
> all are one in thee, for all are thine.
> Alleluia, Alleluia!
> ('For all the saints', William Walsham How, 1864)

Rowan Williams has said that the next stage on from discipleship is not leadership, as most of us assume. Rather it is citizenship. Our worship ought to be training people to be better citizens of this earth, and not just of heaven. And our celebrations of the Eucharist, when we proclaim the Lord's death until he comes, should allow us the reality of present struggle and failure while also lifting our vision away from a kind of heavenly rescue helicopter which will winch us out of all this mess, and towards the glorious banquet when heaven and earth shall have been made new.

Much of the weight of this within *Common Worship* is carried in the Advent material although the way it is presented in *Times and Seasons* is very prescriptive. And in many churches Advent spirituality gets lost in practical preparations for Christmas. A vision for worship that reflects Christ's promises and challenges must be one in which the here and now is understood in the light of eternity. This may well go beyond simply the recovery of Advent.

There is, however, one further implication of eschatological worship. Someone might remark that the Church of England is to all intents and purposes universalist, and some high-profile evangelical leaders have 'come out' and said explicitly that they hold that position. Many parish churches see their role as basically being nice to everyone: one priest said to me recently, 'Of course we're not here to evangelize the village!' Yet when we listen to the teaching of Jesus it is clear that eschatology implies separation: indeed the New Testament is full of contrasts between those who will find themselves 'in' and those who will be 'out'. The way we choose to respond to Jesus in penitence and faith in this life will clearly affect his response to us in the future. If our worship says or implies that everyone who is basically quite nice will be assured of a future in paradise, or that God's love is 'unconditional' (a concept nowhere found in the Bible), we do them a great disservice. Having an eschatological flavour means our worship must call people to heart-searching and repentance. It is a corny cliché to ask people, 'Where will you spend eternity?', but our worship needs to go on asking, and demanding a response.

TO THINK ABOUT

- What are you hoping for?

TO DISCUSS

- How does our worship challenge people to consider the here and now in the light of eternity?

THE END

Like coming to the end of a service, we are at that liminal, transitional point between the dispersal of the gathered assembly and the world into which we go, both as Church and as individuals. Like the church service, this book is no use unless you do something with it. It should lead and provoke you to action, though that may be contemplation, meditation and silence, or renewed Spirit-filled prayer before taking action on a thought that has come as you have been reading or discussing. Remember that everything is connected – look at the links (see Ephesians 4 and Ezekiel 37). You could try pursuing the connections by exploring how the chapters of the book connect and interplay with each other. Belonging affects our caring, which affects how we and others believe and how the Church grows and is built up. And each of these figures in our prayer and worship, in our view of God and our giving glory to God. If that is the result, the book will achieve its purpose and our worship will change: glory to God the Father, Son and Holy Spirit!

INDEX